THE OLD EGYPTIAN FAITH

BY

EDOUARD NAVILLE

Hon. D.C.L , LL.D., Ph.D., Litt.D., Hon. F.S

CORRESPONDENT OF THE INSTITUTE OF FRANCE;
FOREIGN MEMBER OF THE HUNGARIAN ACADEMY OF SCIENCE;
FELLOW OF KING'S COLLEGE, LONDON;
PROFESSOR OF EGYPTOLOGY AT THE UNIVERSITY OF GENEVA

TRANSLATED BY

COLIN CAMPBELL, M.A., D.D.

MINISTER OF DUNDEE PARISH

AUTHOR OF
"THE GARDENER'S TOMB AT THEBES," "TWO THEBAN QUEENS,"
"CRITICAL STUDIES IN ST LUKE'S GOSPEL," "THE FIRST
THREE GOSPELS IN GREEK," ETC.

ISBN: 978-1-63923-710-4

All Rights reserved. No part of this book maybe reproduced without written permission from the publishers, except by a reviewer who may quote brief passages in a review to be printed in a newspaper or magazine.

Printed: February 2023

Published and Distributed By:
Lushena Books
607 Country Club Drive, Unit E
Bensenville, IL 60106
www.lushenabks.com

ISBN: 978-1-63923-710-4

CROWN THEOLOGICAL LIBRARY

VOL. XXX.
NAVILLE'S THE OLD EGYPTIAN FAITH

The Forty-two Gods, who avenge the

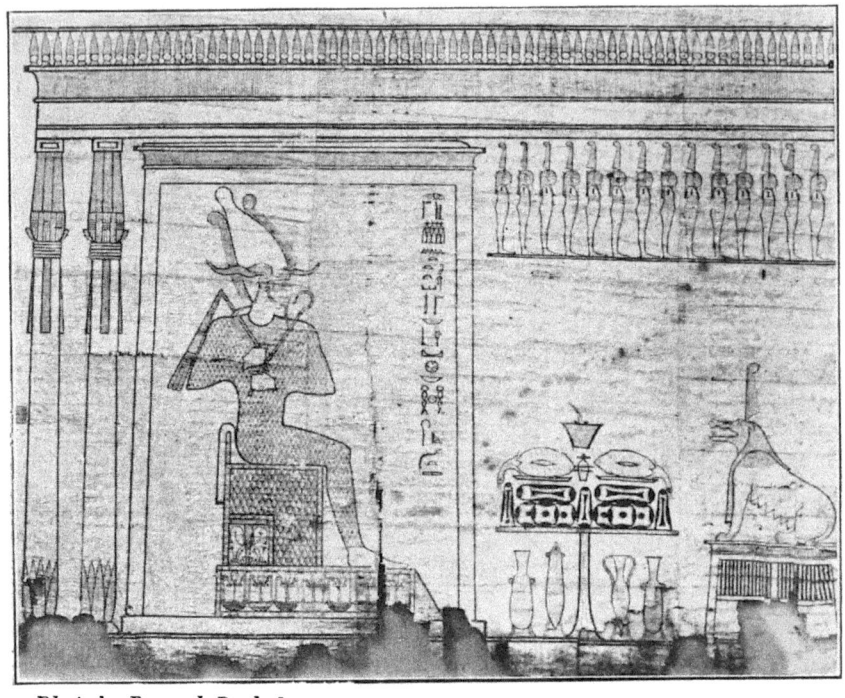

Photo by Brugsch Pasha]

Osiris in his Shrine

Ammit, "The Eater"
(of the condemned).

THE WEIGHING
IN THE HALL

[*Frontispiece.*

Forty-two Trespasses, adored by the Deceased.

[*from a Ptolemaic Papyrus in Cairo*

Thoth recording the Judgment.   Anubis and Horus watching the Balance.   The Deceased supported by the Goddess of Truth

OF THE HEART
OF THE TRUTHS.

PREFACE

THE six Lectures which compose the present volume were the first that were instituted at the Collége de France in terms of the Michonis endowment, and were delivered in 1905.

Their subject—the religion of the old Egyptians—covers too wide a field and raises too many different questions to permit us to make a complete study of it in so small a compass, or to enter into all the discussions to which this religion has given rise. I have accordingly selected six principal topics, the development of which appeared to me to be likely to afford us a general idea of the Egyptian religion, in spite of numerous omissions which the shortness of the time at my disposal rendered inevitable. For this reason I have endeavoured, in this volume, to keep these studies in the character and form of lectures; in this respect I have really made almost no change.

I crave the indulgence of my learned colleagues if in this general review, intended for an ordinary public audience, I have not been able to acknowledge my several obligations to them individually, and to mention their names. Especially am I indebted to the brilliant and instructive investigations of M. Maspero and M. Wiedemann. Others will recognise in the following pages, alongside of my own personal opinions, the fruits of their labours and discoveries, which have now become common property.

My desire being, as far as possible, to imbue my hearers with the spirit of the people whose beliefs we had to study, I have frequently allowed the Egyptians to speak for themselves; hence the large number of translations to be found in the volume, of which in almost every instance I have mentioned the authors.

PREFACE

The first lecture alone is slightly different in character from the rest. It was necessary, at the start, to show who the Egyptians were, and what their origin was; and this involved an examination of the results of recent discoveries in their bearing on questions which are still matters of much controversy.

EDOUARD NAVILLE.

MALAGNY, NEAR GENEVA,
June 1906.

TRANSLATOR'S NOTE

A RE-PERUSAL of Professor Edouard Naville's *La Religion des Anciens Égyptiens*, in Egypt last winter, convinced me that, even after the appearance of the excellent works of Wiedemann, Erman, Budge, and others, in English, on the Egyptian Religion, there was still room for another exposition of the Old Egyptian Faith, such as that which Dr Naville's *Conférences* afforded. Accordingly, I applied to him for permission to translate the Lectures into English—a privilege which he most cordially granted. I can only hope that the result of my pleasant labours, as presented in the following pages, will not only justify Professor Naville's confidence in a humble worker in the vast and ever-expanding field of Egyptian studies—to which he was introduced more than a quarter of a century ago by his old and revered teacher, the late Professor Lushington,—but will also assist in the comprehension of perhaps the most wonderful body—it can hardly be called a system —of religious beliefs that the human mind has ever conceived.

It would be an impertinence on my part to commend Professor Naville's work, either in the domain of religion or of Egyptology generally; I have been only a "sitter at his feet." The history of Egyptian thought and civilisation can never be truly presented to the world without assigning to him a foremost place in the ranks of original investigators. Yet, perhaps, I may be allowed here to state that this little book—little, because its author purposely omitted many otherwise interesting details— seems to me to afford some lucid guiding ideas and principles, not met with in any other work known to me, which go a long way to explain and illuminate the origin and the growth of the religious conceptions of the Egyptians during thousands of years. Even many of the details omitted, which seem to many other writers so important, and which, especially when illustrated, are so captivating to the ordinary reader, will find their explanation in the principles here laid down. On many points, too, it will be found that the author advances opinions different from many that are current, especially in recent histories and other accounts; but it is needless to say that Dr Naville can always support his positions by arguments and proofs which even protagonists like himself, not to mention amateur skirmishers, will find it hard, if not impossible, to overthrow. His judgments are cautious because they are based on full knowledge; he is accurate and clear in his statements because he knows how easy it is to slip into misstatements for the sake of effect; and in a field where the play of fancy and imagination is so alluring, he is commendably reserved and sober, without being unsympathetic. I desire, in this reference, to draw special attention to a note, written at my request, which will be found at the end of Chapter III., on the brilliant, if brief, reform accomplished in religion and art by that extraordinary genius, the Pharaoh Amenhotep IV., Khu-en-aten, a portrait of whom, from a slab found by the translator in Luqsor Temple in 1906, is included in this volume.

The illustrations are almost entirely from photographs taken by the translator on the spot. With Dr Naville's consent, I have introduced three photographs of scenes from the discovery of the marvellous Hathor Cow and Shrine at Thebes on February 7, 1906, when my wife and I had the good fortune to be present. In one of the pictures, taken soon after the discovery, Dr Naville is seen beside the Shrine, which, with the Cow, is now in the Cairo Museum of Egyptian Antiquities. It is a unique representation of Hathor as a Cow. The frontispiece, illustrating the Weighing of the Heart, is from a photograph taken specially for this translation, by Brugsch Pasha, of the

Cairo Museum. It is from a Ptolemaic papyrus in the Museum, and has never before been published. Unfortunately, it is too long to be reproduced in one length. My thanks are due to him for this picture; as well as to the Trustees of the British Museum, for permission, through the kindness of Dr Budge, to reproduce a scene from the Papyrus of Hunefer, representing the worship of the Osiris-Dad as the Rising Sun.

The translator hopes that these pages, in which he has endeavoured to present Dr Naville's meaning faithfully, will not only be of service to the traveller in Egypt, but also to the student of comparative theology and religion. A glance at the contents of the chapters will suggest to the latter some subjects which will give him food for thought.

C. C.

EDINBURGH,
October 26, 1909.

CONTENTS

I

Origin of the Ancient Egyptians: Not Negroes: Their Prehistoric Pottery Pictures: Their Civilisation was African: Who was Mena? The Invaders: From S. Arabia: Egyptian Orientation: The so-called Royal Tombs of Abydos, mere Funerary Chapels: Slate Palettes: The Primitive Royal Name: The Falcon Kings: The King a Horus, and Divine: Mena or Menes, the First King, a Foreigner: The *Ka* and the Fan: A Hierarchy: Mena's Name not yet Found: Agriculture the Basis of Civilisation: The Nile: Building with Brick and Stone: Egyptian Architecture Unique: Animals: Papyrus Plant: Vine Culture: Writing: Metal-working Imported: The Horites: Horus and Set: "The Opener of the Ways": Anthropomorphism: Possible Relations with Babylon . . 1-50

II

Methods of Burial: The so-called Embryonic Posture: Dismemberment of the Body: Wiedemann's Theory: The *Ka*: Secondary Burial: Revolt against Dismemberment: Life of the *Ka*: Personality: Body, Ka, Soul, Shadow, Heart, etc.: Prospects of the Dead: Tombs of the Old Empire: The Ideal Life: The *Mástaba*: Chamber for the *Ka*: The Stele in the Tomb: No other Religious Object: Importance of the Double or *Ka*: Ancient Worship: Idealised Terrestrial Bliss: The Pyramids are but Tombs: Mariette's Discovery:

PAGES

Pyramid Religious Texts: The First Pyramid Inscription: The Osiris Myth: Every Dead King an Osiris: Pyramid Texts for the King only: Book of the Dead for All: Mummification: The Temples are Mortuary Chapels: Hatshepsu's Temple and Tomb: Ramesseum: The Douat: Forms of the Book "Am Douat": The Night-Sun's Journey: The Escort of Ra: Those who accompany Ra: Those who do not: The Soldiers of Ra, and the Enemies of Ra: Re-birth of the Sun (Ra): The Serpent called "The Life of the Gods": The Friends of Ra: *Ushabti* Figures: The Mortuary Chamber 51–103

III

The Doctrine of Heliopolis: Egyptian Religion Unsystematic: The Egyptians could not forget, either in Religion or in Art: No Fixed Doctrine, therefore no Heresy: The Ancient Heliopolis (On), the Religious Capital: The Ennead of the Gods of Heliopolis: The Cosmic Gods: Their Descent: Osiris the most interesting God: The only one with a touch of Morality: The *Dad* Symbol, the Skeleton of Osiris: Set and Nephthys: Set represents the Wild Animal-world: History of the Creation: "The Adoration of Ra": The Seventy-five Forms: "Litany of the Sun": Henotheism: Pantheism: The Theban Doctrine: The Theban Triad, Amon, Mut, and Khons: Hymns to Amon: Amon not a Creative God: "The Decrees of Amon": Pantheism again: Colleges of Priests: Priestly Power: The Aten Worship and Hymns: Amenhotep IV., Khu-en-aten: Pantheism of the Aten Hymns: Khu-en-aten's Reform political rather than religious in its aim: Note on Khu-en-aten's Revolt 104–158

IV

The Book of the Dead: Not a Unity any more than the Book of Psalms: Magic at its Root: Should be called "Book of Coming out FROM THE DAY" instead of "BY DAY": Its Chapters and their Titles: The Meaning

CONTENTS

of "The Triumphant One": Origin of the Book: Old Empire Fragments of the Book: Chapter XVII. perhaps the Oldest: The Saite Recension: Difficulties of the Book: Its Introductory Hymns to Osiris and Ra: Reconstruction or Reconstitution of Osiris: Power of Thoth: Magical Virtue of the Words of the Book: Incoherent Doctrines: Myth of Osiris: Transmigration of Souls: Garden of Aalou: The "Answerers": The Judgment of the Soul: Repudiation of certain Trespasses, a Preliminary Confession: The Weighing of the Heart before Osiris; the Forty-two Gods and the Forty-two Trespasses: The Confession and the Decalogue compared: The Sentence: Conscience: Future Bliss: Dialogue of a Man with his Soul: Egyptian Pessimism, *Carpe Diem*: A Woman's Wail in the Next World: A Better Hope 159–207

V

Anthropomorphism in the Egyptian Religion: Egyptian Myths, and Greek: The Myth of the Destruction of Mankind: Origin of Sacrifice: Creation of the Heaven (Sky) and the Earth: More Incoherence: The Magical Use of Myths: An Egyptian Deluge: Why Swine were forbidden to be Sacrificed to Horus: Myth of Ra and Isis the Enchantress: Her Device to gain the Knowledge of Ra's Name: More Magical Myths: Miracle of Healing by Thoth: Anthropomorphic Myths: The Complaint of the Sphinx, who begs to be cleared of the Sand: The Relations of Gods and Men —a System of Bargaining: Prayer of Rameses II to Amon: His Claims on Amon: A Healing Image: The Story of the Possessed Princess: Speaking Statues: The Fellah's Religion a Nature-cult . . 208–263

VI

Rites and Ceremonies: The Sovereign's Divine Birth: Queen Hatshepsu's and King Amenhotep III.'s Divine Birth: The Enthronement of Queen Hatshepsu at Dêr el

	PAGES
Bahri: Her Presentation to the People: Associated with her Father, Thothmes I., on the Throne: The Worship of the Monarch, even during Life: Determining the Royal Style and Names: Royal Duties to the Gods: The Founding of a Temple: The Sed Festivals: Deification of the King: The King always Divine: Kings and Ordinary Mortals: Cult of the King in Life: Cult of other Divinities: Rituals of Abydos and Thebes: The Daily Service: A Glance of the God might be Fatal: Sacrifice, and the Egyptian Account of the Origin of Sacrifice: Human Sacrifice in Egypt: Amenhotep II.'s Slaughter of Seven Princes: Description of a Theban Tomb where Human Sacrifice is alleged: M. Maspero's Theory untenable: Human Sacrifice possibly practised on Extraordinary Occasions: Its Burlesque in Ptolemaic Times: Wealth of the Egyptian Ceremonial: The Latest Cults: Differences between the Old and the New Customs and Inscriptions on the Temples: Excessive Development of Magic: Hybrid Divinities: Dawn of Christianity: The so-called Hermetic Books: End of the Egyptian Religion: The Farewell Lament of a Faithful Soul	264–319

Principal Authorities 320, 321

LIST OF ILLUSTRATIONS

The Weighing of the Heart. (Two Parts.) From a Ptolemaic Papyrus . . . . *Frontispiece*

	PAGE
The Hathor Shrine and Cow, with Professor Naville, the Discoverer	
Horus name of King, with epithet DEN . . .	18
Thothmes III. worshipping Ptah, Patron of the Blacksmiths	41
The so-called Embryonic Posture in Burial . .	53
The Sun-God in his Boat at Night	91
The Horus of Edfou	108
Isis and Nephthys adoring Osiris as the Rising Sun	126
Thothmes III. worshipping Amon Ra . . .	138
Amenhotep IV. (Khu-en-aten)	151
Khons-Neferhotep, Mut, and Amon worshipped by the King	250
Amenhotep II. being suckled by the Hathor Cow .	266
Horus name of Hatshepsut, " rich in *kas* " . .	271

LIST OF ILLUSTRATIONS

	PAGE
Sety I. offering Maat (Truth) to Osiris . . .	292
Man in Skin, Tomb of Paheri	300
Man in Skin, Tomb of Renni	302
Man in Skin, Tomb of Sen-nofer	305
Man in Skin, Tomb of Menna	306

[*To face page* 1

[*Photo by Translator*

The Hathor Shrine and Cow, February 7, 1906,
with Professor Naville.

THE
OLD EGYPTIAN FAITH

I

WHO were the Egyptians? To what race did they belong? Were they autochthonous, native to the soil, or were they invaders who brought with them from their foreign home that interesting civilisation of theirs, with its sharply defined character,—a civilisation which, outwardly at least, seems to have remained essentially the same for more than four thousand years?

These are some of the questions which have for long confronted all who are engaged in Egyptian studies. They have forced themselves all the more strikingly on the attention from the fact that the Egyptian civilisation seems to emerge quite suddenly, without any previous preparation, or anything to herald its coming. At the very outset it appeared in all its own beauty, a beauty imperfect and inferior perhaps, but still of a kind which seems not to lack the elements of growth and development. It is true that it preferred not to turn these elements to any or much account; for, with periods of alternating splendour and decay, it remained throughout its history much the same as it had been at its first appearance. But the question recurs, what was the source of origin of these first manifestations, and how many centuries had to elapse before the civilisation reached that point?

For a long period it was believed that the enigma would remain insoluble, and that all our efforts to raise the veil of the impenetrable mystery would be baffled. But during the last decade light has dawned and broken forth from this old land of Egypt, from its very sand, which has so affectionately preserved so many treasures of antiquity, and which, we are convinced, still safely holds in its bosom a rich harvest, if not for ourselves, at least for our children.

The recent excavations of Amélineau, Morgan, Petrie, Quibell, and others have revealed to us that, as far back as we can go, there existed in Egypt a primitive population with a degree of culture which had not emerged from what we call the Stone Age. It was clearly an African race; the same people who, in later times, were called Libyans, and are represented in our day by the peoples of North Africa, like the Berbers.

When we speak of Libyans or Berbers, we must not think that we are dealing with a negro race; quite the contrary. "I set aside, at the very beginning, the negro race," says Dr Fouquet, who has made a careful study of the craniology of that remote epoch, and who, without making an absolute pronouncement as to the origin of the Egyptian race, affirms that the people had straight hair, sometimes even fair in colour, and that there is an entire absence of that prognathism or prominence of jaw which, with woolly hair, is the most marked characteristic of the negro type.

Some rude paintings which adorn the pottery found in the tombs of this epoch afford us a glimpse of the manner of life of this aboriginal race, as I shall call them. In the first place, they were huntsmen; bows and arrows provided them with food, for they do not seem to have been much in love with agriculture. And if we may judge from the rather uncouth drawings found on these earthenware articles—drawings which have been interpreted in different ways,—their wicker-work dwellings stood in enclosures surrounded by stakes, intended primarily to protect the inhabitants from wild animals. Within these enclosures we see men, bow in hand, and women, as well as several kinds of desert animals, which the bowmen seem not only to have tamed, but also to have domesticated. I note especially different kinds of gazelles and antelopes, large herds of which rich Egyptians, centuries afterwards, loved to possess. In later days, when more useful animals replaced these creatures, they were allowed to return to their wild state. Within these enclosures of the primitive people we see neither cattle, nor asses, nor sheep which would have been brought from abroad by the conquering race when they subjugated the indigenous population. We can recognise, however, in spite of the imperfect drawing and painting, different kinds of birds, especially ostriches, which seem to have held a large place in the poultry-yards of these primitive peoples. Generally speaking, the huts shown in the enclosures are two in number, one on either side of the door. Boats propelled by rowers or by sails prove that the people knew how to navigate: these boats were most probably used mainly for fishing. Nothing as yet reveals that these aborigines practised any form of cult, except a kind of standard, set up above one of the huts. It was perhaps either the totem or the sacred animal of the family over whose dwelling it stood.

Now this culture or civilisation, so rudimentary in its nature, is an African culture. It has been styled Libyan, a name which stands for nothing definite.

The Libyans or the Africans in old Egypt included different hordes or tribes; it seems, indeed, that in the time of the fifth dynasty a white African population occupied the region adjoining what is now the Sudan, namely, Darfour and Kordofan. These peoples, whom we find afterwards on the western frontier of Egypt, whence they several times menaced the kingdom of the Pharaohs, are called the Tamahou or Tehennu. We see that they practised tatooing, a fact which we can establish also from one or two small figures of the oldest epoch; and they also adorned their heads with ostrich feathers, as did the primitive bowmen.

In my opinion, these white African people

bore also another name, that of Anou, which means archers; and from Nubia as far as Sinai we find them always regarded as the enemies of the conquering race.

Thus the basis of the Egyptian population was African, and Caucasian in type; this race appears to have spread much further to the south than it afterwards did, and subsequently to have been driven northwards by the negroes. This old African people has still its representatives to-day, in the Berbers and Kabyles, for example, amongst whom we find almost the same arts, especially the pottery, which we meet with in the prehistoric epoch.

Now, did these Anou possess towns? It is interesting that the city which was the religious centre or metropolis of Egypt, afterwards called Heliopolis, bears in Egyptian the very same name of An. In fact, one of the names of Egypt is "the two lands of An." The oldest religious myths, too, carry us back to Heliopolis. It is quite possible, then, that the conquerors of whom we shall shortly speak had established their own cult in the old metropolis of the indigenous people, which was then perhaps but a simple village, but which continued to the latest times to be regarded with the greatest reverence, and maintained all its prestige to the end. For, according to the mythological geography, the city of cities, corresponding to our heavenly Jerusalem, was the city of An.

The Greek historians and the oldest hieroglyphic lists tell us that the first historical king was called Mena or Menes. It is certain that with his advent something happened in Egypt which worked a great change in the whole state of the country : it appears, indeed, that he was the first to unite under his sceptre the tribes or hordes scattered up and down the river. Was Mena a native of the soil? did he belong to that African stock of which we have spoken, or was he himself a foreigner? Was he the conqueror, and did he belong to the race who subdued the aborigines, who were settled on the banks of the river before him? To these questions we are unable to give a positive answer; but, as we shall try to establish, it seems quite probable that he was of the conquering race, for all the authorities which allude to him are at one in declaring that it was he who introduced into the country what we should call civilisation. Clearly he represented a new element which developed and transformed the old stock of the native population, which up to this time had been rather backward.

We must now attempt to discover whence came this foreign element. If we consult not only the hieroglyphic documents, but those relating either to the people of Israel or to old Babylon, we shall find that, along the Red Sea, on both shores, in Arabia as well as in Africa, there stretches a region which bore different names, one of which is Kush—often incorrectly rendered Ethiopia,—and another, Pount, very common in the hieroglyphic inscriptions, or even Ta-nouter, the divine land, its more frequent designation. It seems that the district which in primitive times bore this name was Arabia of the South, and it was from it that the populations migrated who were settled on the African shore. This Arabia of the South seems to have been peopled by a race whose personal appearance at that remote epoch we are ignorant of, but of whom, at a later age, when they inhabited the African portion of the country of Pount, we possess some portraits. They were men of an aquiline type, with pointed beard, and silky hair, sometimes tied up with a head-band or fillet or decked out with an ostrich feather; and they wear a cincture like the Egyptians: altogether, a race in all respects similar to the dwellers on the Nile, though the paintings which show them are later by several thousand years than the date of the sojourn of the conquerors of the Nile valley in the south of Arabia. The only difference worth pointing out is a difference of colour—the people of Pount being painted in a deeper red than the Egyptians. It is, then, from the south of Arabia that we bring the foreign element, and it belonged to the same race as the Africans, who conquered the first occupants of the country, and who brought them their civilisation.

By what route did they come? Opinions differ considerably on this point. It has been said, by Lepsius for instance, that they entered by the isthmus of Suez, but this point of view seems now abandoned. They must have crossed the Red Sea; it is difficult to say where. Petrie believes that they landed at a place now called Kosseir Harbour, and that they passed through the Wady Hamamat, which would have taken them towards the town of Keneh, in Middle Egypt, a little to the north of Thebes. For myself, I cannot help thinking that they crossed the Red Sea further to the south, and landed perhaps somewhere in the region of Massowah, or even on the coast of Abyssinia. This opinion agrees with the data of the classical authors, of whom I will quote only one, Diodorus Siculus. He says: "The Ethiopians affirm that Egypt is one of their colonies. The very soil is brought down from their country by the deposits of the Nile. There are striking resemblances between the customs and laws of the two countries"; and he mentions several instances, like the following: "the kings have the same costume, and the uræus serpent adorns their crown." I will confine myself to this quotation; I might produce others, for, according to the Greek authors, it was clearly from Ethiopia the Egyptians came. There is, in all this, it appears to me, a distant allusion to the migration from Arabia, of which we have spoken, and which would be first arrested at the banks of the river, in Upper Egypt.

We can, however, offer even better evidence, especially the way in which the Egyptian takes his bearings. He always turns to the south, the west being thus on his right hand, and the east on his left. We must not think of this as implying that he walks towards the south, thus following the direction indicated to him by his ancestors. I believe that the explanation of it is quite different. In the mythological traditions, Horus, the king of Egypt, is regarded as coming down the Nile and conquering Egypt, which was under Set. It is, then, natural for the Egyptian to turn towards the god; he turns at the same time towards the Nile, and he pays homage to the great river whose beneficent waters bring him his means of sustenance and suffer him to live. Besides, it is a fact beyond all doubt that, in the division into two parts, which even in the most remote epochs appears whenever Egypt is mentioned, Egypt of the South—Upper Egypt—is always named first, she has always the precedence and the pre-eminence over the other. The kings of Upper Egypt are mentioned before those of Lower Egypt. The word king, or royal, is sufficient in itself to indicate the king of Upper Egypt. In certain sacrifices, too, when in place of slaughtering two bulls one will suffice, the one slain is that of Upper Egypt. The national character, also, has always been more marked in Upper than in Lower Egypt. I believe, therefore, that this kind of predilection of the Egyptians for the south arose out of a tradition reminding them that the south had been their first place of settlement.

These emigrants, who came from the south of Arabia, always advancing further north, and following the course of the river, passed the First Cataract and emerged from the region where the mountains and the desert sand reach the Nile; then, the cataract left behind, they found themselves in a wide valley, inundated every year by the river, and covered with luxuriant vegetation. Here it was that they gave themselves up to agriculture, which became the pathway that led them to an advanced state of civilisation.

The degree of culture possessed by these invaders is known to us by the excavations made in recent years by Amélineau, Petrie, and Morgan in different parts of Egypt. They came upon buildings, sometimes underground, composed of a central chamber round

SO-CALLED ROYAL TOMBS (ABYDOS) 15

which were ranged rows of narrow rooms, all of them containing vases, remains of furniture, and especially amphoræ with earthen stoppers bearing an impression made by a cylinder on the clay while it was still soft. These buildings have been called tombs, and even royal tombs; indeed, in all the recent works which deal with them they are called the Royal Tombs of Abydos. The most famous is the one that some would fain associate with Menes, situated in a locality called Negadah. I cannot fall in with this view; I look on these buildings as funerary chapels in which a certain cult was rendered to the dead who were buried at some depth underneath, or somewhere in the neighbourhood.

But these buildings are not the only monuments that remain to us of that remote period. We possess also what are known as palettes, in schist, of different sizes. Of only one of them do we know the place of origin. The largest are 74 and 76 centimetres in length, and are scarcely more than 2 centimetres thick. They are generally covered on both sides with sculptures, and it is not impossible that a thin plating of gold was added as an enrichment of the decorations. In the middle of one face of the palette is a little round hollow, which some authorities would regard as a place for grinding colours. I believe that the purpose of this hollow is quite different, especially if we have regard to the representations which surround it. It was meant to hold the emblem of a king or a god —an emblem perhaps conical in form, either a precious stone or a piece of wood, in the shape of a cone or pyramid. The majority of these palettes are ornamented only with representations of men or of animals, but there is a small number of them which bear real inscriptions in hieroglyphics, and that in hieroglyphics quite similar to those that we shall meet at a later period. We must, then, admit that the writing as we know it was imported by the conquering foreigners. But when I say imported, is it the proper word to use? Were they already in possession of this script before they set out from Arabia? I cannot go so far as this: I incline, on the contrary, to the belief that the writing was developed after they had occupied the valley of the Nile. For it is certain that the writing has a very pronounced Egyptian character: we never find it mixed up with a foreign element.

The pottery, palettes, ivories, jar-sealings or stoppers which have been found in the excavations in different places, but especially at Abydos, allow us to form an approximate idea of what the civilisation of these foreigners was.

And first, let us begin with the kings, and note that their names are written in quite a special way, and in a framework always the same. At the top of the group we see a bird of prey, which has been long called a hawk, and which M. Loret has decided is a falcon, the peregrine falcon. This bird is perched on an oblong rectangle, which is often described as a banner, and which ends at the bottom in a collection of lines recalling the front of a funerary chapel, the door by which the double of the deceased is supposed to go in and out.

Horus name of king, with epithet DEN.

At the top of the rectangle, and under the falcon's feet, is a space in which are inscribed one or two hieroglyphic signs, signifying some characteristic epithet of the king or the dominant quality by which he wished specially to be distinguished. The group is thus not even the name of the Pharaoh — the prenomen by which he was designated,—it is a qualification or title—the first title, or the first element of the complicated protocol which forms a royal name. But the fact that the kings of the first dynasties are cited almost always by this qualification or description and not by their prenomen, yet affords us information of the utmost consequence. The ancient kings are thus all of them falcons, men falcons, the companions of the falcon; we are told, in fact, that this bird is the emblem, the standard of the tribe to which they belong. Now, the falcon (in Egyptian, *heru*), from its first appearance in this way down to the time when the beliefs of ancient Egypt vanished, is the god Horus—whether he is represented under the form of the bird, or has the likeness of a man with a falcon's head. Further, the Egyptian word *heru*, the falcon, is also an Arabic word; and this brings us back again to the opinion we have advanced above, that the original home of the conquering Egyptians must be sought for in Arabia.

Thus, it was the companions of Horus that brought civilisation to the land of Egypt when they conquered the indigenous African race that peopled it. This fact, which we gather from the oldest monuments, is confirmed either by legends or by the reports of the Greek historians. According to several chronologies Horus is the last of the gods who ruled over Egypt as the predecessors of the historical kings; and in the hieroglyphic inscriptions the " companions or followers of Horus" represent the legendary epoch—the period called by the Greeks the epoch of the Manes—demi-gods, — though, however, they were mortals. Everything that transpired in the time of the " followers of Horus" represented to the ancient Egyptians events of such hoary antiquity that it could not be measured. A design, found in a brick wall, which was drawn at the time of the companions of Horus, goes back to prehistoric times. Thus, at the very beginning, on the threshold of history, we find Horus and his companions, a clan, a tribe who had the falcon as their sacred animal or their god; every king is himself a Horus, and in the oldest inscriptions that we possess, the king is not designated by his prenomen, or personal name, he is *a Horus* with this or that qualification or description added. This is the important fact which we must bear in mind, namely, that the king is in very deed the double of the sacred bird of the tribe, and, moreover, that by thus establishing his divine nature he is invested with an authority from which no one could escape. If we remember, too, that all the sovereigns of Egypt, even the Roman emperors, reckoned the Horus title among those bestowed upon them at their accession, we must recognise that we are here face to face with a tradition of extraordinary vitality, since it lasted more than four thousand years. In all ages the idea of royalty, and consequently of power and authority, was associated with the name of Horus: "to sit upon the throne of Horus" was to enter into possession of all the rights which royalty conferred; and the king became, *ipso facto*, a divine being.

In the epoch of the Macedonian kings the conquest of Egypt by Horus formed the subject of a long narrative, engraved on one of the walls of the temple of Edfou. By that time, owing to the modifications which had taken place in the religion and the mythology, Horus was no longer merely the falcon whom the conquering tribe had followed in the dim and distant past, he had become the local god of Edfou, in whose honour a magnificent temple was erected, served by a large college of priests, and the great object was to glorify the god of the locality. Accordingly, the legend recounted how his father, Ra Harmachis, reigned in Nubia, and how in the three hundred and sixty-third year of his reign he embarked in a ship, followed by soldiers without number, in order to make a descent on Egypt, at that time in the possession of Set and his companions. Starting from Edfou, and coming down stream, his son Horus fought numerous battles, the various episodes of which are enshrined in the names of the places where he reported his victories. Though certainly we must not look for history in this legend, we may nevertheless conclude from it that even in the time of the Ptolemies the belief was still held that Egypt had been conquered by the followers of Horus, and that they had set out from Nubia, where they had been long settled. For us this sojourn in Nubia means but the first stage in a migration which originated in Arabia.

The hieroglyphic lists of the kings as well as the Greek historians inform us that Menes was the first king. The latter often refer to this king as coming from This, a district in Middle Egypt, in the near neighbourhood of what was afterwards called Abydos. Hence the time of Menes and his immediate successors is styled the Thinite epoch. He went down stream and founded Memphis, on the borders of the Delta. Mention is made of wars waged by him outside of Egypt, of works undertaken for damming the Nile, and of progress of all sorts making for civilisation. Diodorus contributes this extraordinary story: "Menes instructed his people to fear the gods, and to offer sacrifices to them; he also taught them how to use tables and beds and costly stuffs—in a word, he introduced luxurious and sumptuous living. And some generations after, when King Tnephactus, the father of

Bocchoris the Wise, in an expedition against the Arabs, was compelled, in consequence of the failure of supplies in a desolate and destitute country, to put up with, for a whole day, the coarsest and most wretched fare, he found it perfectly delightful, and cursed the luxury of his predecessor, and gave vent to imprecations on the king who had first set the example of such magnificence. Moreover, he applied himself so thoroughly to make an entire change in his food, drink, and bed, that he commanded the priests to inscribe his imprecations in the sacred books of the temple of Jupiter at Thebes. And this seems to me to be the reason why the glory and the honour paid to Menes did not endure to the latest times." In this, however, Diodorus was mistaken, for the cult of Menes lasted for a very long time.

Menes is assuredly the first sovereign whom the Egyptians regarded as king of Egypt. There is no doubt whatever on this point, as the lists preserved to us are quite distinct.

MENA A FOREIGNER

I am accordingly unable to accept theories which have been recently put forward as to pre-Menite or pre-dynastic kings. When we find a king like Rameses II. drawing up a list of sovereigns who had reigned before him, and going back to the beginning in order to show what a numerous and glorious line of monarchs had preceded him upon the throne, we may be sure that he would begin with the first, or with him whom the annalists of his time accepted as the first. Had there been other kings before Menes, Rameses would not have failed to have named them.

Now Mena or Menes belongs to the foreigners or that tribe of Horus who subjugated the indigenous race and ended by amalgamating with them so as to form one people, just as it happened with the Normans and the Saxons in Great Britain. Though Menes is said to have founded Memphis, it was, however, in Abydos, in Middle Egypt, that the capital of the first kings remained, where have been found, up to the present, the majority of the monuments, especially those which have been called the tombs, belonging to this remote age.

A careful study of the objects discovered in these tombs—which, for my part, I must continue to call funerary chapels, that is, the portion of the tomb set apart for worship and not the place where the deceased was buried—will show that even then Egyptian civilisation was of a very advanced order. It does not differ much from that which afterwards existed when the contemporaries of the Memphite kings had those magnificent tombs excavated which excite the admiration of travellers. From the very beginning hieroglyphic script is in use; it is doubtless less developed than it was later, but the signs are just the same and have the same value. We can read almost all the inscriptions impressed on the clay stoppers of the jars, or graven on the ivory plaques, or even on the palettes or maces. And the inscription, just as in later times, is often the accompaniment of a sculptured or painted scene, of which it is the explanation.

These scenes and inscriptions already supply us with a correct idea of the degree of civilisation attained by these old Pharaohs; they built with brick, but also with stone; and the ceremonies connected with the foundation of a building are already seen, if in a rudimentary state. If the matter in hand is the marking out of a temple boundary, the king takes a hoe or mattock and traces its lines on the ground, while someone pours sand or gravel into the furrow which he has made, in order to define the impression, just as was done, several thousand years later, by a Roman Emperor at Denderah. Behind the king are the fan-bearers. The fans must not be regarded simply as means of supplying fresh and cool air to the king; they have chiefly a symbolical signification, as representing a vital element of his personality — the emblem of what is called the shade or the double — <u>the ka</u>,—of which any person could have several, and which was an indispensable element of personality. Wanting this double, the person was annihilated. Thus the double became the protecting genius who always accompanied the king, and without whom he would not be a complete being. The fan, the emblem of this double, is thus a talisman to preserve the king, even in war, and as such it is seen behind his chariot when he goes into battle.

We thus see that this collection of symbolical or mystical ideas which we find running throughout the whole of Egyptian antiquity already existed at the period of the Thinite kings. There are, besides, other examples of it. Before the king are borne in procession four standards, two of which are crowned with falcons, a third with a jackal, or rather a dog, and the fourth with an emblem which became the representation of the god Khons. These standards, as M. Loret has brought out, were at one time hieroglyphic names of divinities, emblems of tribes, and afterwards became the designations of the nomes or provinces which composed Egypt. We come across these standards in religious ceremonies or in festivals through the whole course of Egyptian antiquity. Thus, among the first descendants of the Horus tribes we can discern the first instances of the outward manifestations of the cult, and of all that rather fantastic religious pomp which afterwards assumed such an extraordinary development.

As we have already mentioned, there was at this period an administrative hierarchy of priests of different orders and functions, and also a division of the soil, or economic organisation, for we find certain lands named as properties belonging to funerary chapels or tombs. Storehouses receive the rents in kind —the produce of these lands, or the offerings that were brought. And if we turn to the department of industry or art, we discover amongst the contemporaries of the Thinites great facility in working such hard material as rock crystal. Sculpture has already made its appearance, for we possess two or three statues which can be referred to that remote time. Some fragments of articles of furniture which have been preserved, such as ivory feet of tables and chairs, might be attributed to the best epoch of Egyptian art. The weapons of the king are the same as they were later; his maces are adorned with the same sculptured scenes, in which the sovereign's headdress is now the diadem of the north, now that of the south, just as a Rameses or a Psammetichus might be crowned. On some of the schist palettes the king clubs his enemies, or celebrates a great festival; on others he is seen following the chase of the desert animals. These palettes were sometimes, as in the case of that of the king whose name I read as Boëthos, *objets de luxe*, and were not the work of a young or a rude people. Without a doubt the civilisation we see there came in with the foreign conquering element; but what the conquerors did find among the indigenous Africans was the native earthenware or pottery, together with great facility in making certain articles in stone, such as vases, even of large dimensions, and flint implements. But as to what I should call the intellectual factor in civilisation—anything that rises above mere manual labour, especially anything relating to a religious cult—of this we can find no trace among the native race who peopled the cemeteries styled prehistoric.

Here, then, we come face to face with a question which always confronts us in Egyptian studies. We imagined we had disposed of it and found an answer to it, but we had only pushed the difficulty further back. It is perfectly clear that the evidences of Egyptian civilisation did not appear for the first time at the epoch of the Pyramids, as was believed ten years ago; for we have since learned that contemporaries of Menes, or his immediate successors, if not Menes himself—whose name we have not yet indisputably found on any contemporary monument—had arrived at a degree of culture very similar to that to which the kings of the historic epochs had attained. We have merely pushed the starting-point several centuries back, or, to adopt Egyptian chronological terms, from the fourth to the first dynasty. But if this first dynasty came, as we believe, from a foreign country; and if, after setting out from Arabia, it crossed the Red Sea to reach the Nile and establish itself for good at the head of the valley of the Great River, we must ask if it also carried with it this civilisation from Arabia, and if so, how comes it that we can discover no traces of it on the way at any stage of the journey? How does it happen that it is only in Egypt we first find it with its characteristics so definitely marked?

If we study the question more closely we shall not be slow to recognise that Egyptian culture in all its features has been determined by the nature of the country where it developed, and consequently that it could hardly have been born outside of the Nile valley. The civilisation is essentially agricultural in its origins; it arises, like the majority of civilisations, from the tilling of the ground. Let us dwell, then, for a little on the interesting feature of the nature of the country, so different from what we find elsewhere in the world. First of all, the whole country is the creation, or, as Herodotus says, the gift of the Great River. The Nile, we know, has a level which varies almost every day. It has no normal depth which it maintains for any prolonged period: it rises and falls unceasingly. At the summer solstice it is lowest; it then begins to rise, and this goes on for almost a hundred days; then some days after, it begins to fall again for eight months. As the waters fall and the fields begin to get uncovered, the inhabitants of the country go forth and sow; after which the harvest comes in the spring months. We understand how, in these circumstances, the Egyptians had only three seasons. They had various years, the tropical year, the vague solar year of three hundred and sixty-five days, and, as Brugsch shows with some reason, a lunar year. But what was, in practice, bound to be the true calendar of the rural population, was the movement of the Nile, in the rising and falling phases of the inundation.

The Egyptian was not slow to notice that the Nile mud, sun-dried, was an easy substance to work, and also very durable, especially in so dry a climate. No great effort of the imagination was needed to hit on brick-making; it was only a matter of cutting the mud out, there was no need to bake it. Egyptian bricks have always been, and are to this day, crude or sun-dried bricks: the burned or baked brick was imported into Egypt by the Romans. The action of fire is necessary in countries where there is no binding matter in the clay. Egyptian building was at first of brick and wood; it was only later that stone was used, and then only for fine buildings, especially for temples. It does not appear as if at any epoch any large use of stone was made for dwelling-houses, or even for palaces. The monarchs of the East loved to erect their own habitations, each for himself; they did not feel bound either to inhabit the houses of their fathers, or to transmit to their descendants those which they themselves had reared, and so these edifices had to be erected quickly.

In the tombs of the Thinite epoch we can trace the transition from brick to stone. In this respect Egypt was singularly favoured, as building materials are plentiful and of splendid quality. It was sandstone that was first used, easy to work, and to be had in Upper Egypt, at Silsilis and its neighbourhood; and of it all the great buildings at Thebes were constructed. Then came a fine white limestone, soft enough to work, and capable of taking on colour, and excellently adapted for the sculpture of hieroglyphics. Various kinds of granite were also employed: the black, which came from the quarries lying between the Nile and the Red Sea; and the famous red granite of Aswan, that superb stone, in frequent use in all periods, and capable of receiving a very fine polish and even of being worked with great delicacy. Nothing was easier than the transition from brick to such excellent materials, lying ready to the hands of the inhabitants. We can thus easily understand how the Egyptians became builders, and were not slow to become so, from the time they settled in the Nile valley, lying as it does between two mountain ramparts which furnished them with all the stones they needed. Edifice construction is certainly the branch of civilisation which they cultivated the most. In this respect, indeed, they have surpassed all other nations of antiquity; and it was on it also they set the highest store themselves. When a king wished to appraise himself, he might speak in vague terms of his conquests, his power, and of his having extended the bounds of his empire to the beginning of the world at the south or to the marshes of the north; but all these are but conventional expressions repeated by sovereign after sovereign. He becomes, however, much more precise when he speaks of his buildings, which are to endure as long as the heavens. In anything pertaining to Egyptian architecture it is impossible to detect a single trace of foreign influence: it is an art wholly native to the country, and determined entirely by the special conditions of the land in which it had its birth.

We have mentioned above that in the earliest representations domestic animals do not appear, but only wild animals, animals of the desert. Latterly, much attention has been given by naturalists to the study of mummified animals; and they have propounded the question whether these animals, particularly sheep and cattle, were really of African origin, or were imported from Asia. The experts have arrived at no unanimous conclusion. It would seem quite probable that several varieties of domestic animals came from abroad, probably from Asia; but that others are really members of the African fauna, and that in Africa they must have been domesticated. If the conquering Horites had brought the domestic animals with them from Asia, it would have been surprising if they had not also brought the horse, which is never seen on the ancient sculptures: he appears only after the great Asiatic invasion of the Hyksos, who probably came from Mesopotamia.

Of the sacred animals, all of which are indigenous, it is curious to find that one of the most venerated has vanished from the fauna of Egypt, namely, the white ibis, the bird of the god Thoth. The same fate has overtaken a plant which the Egyptians used in great quantities, the papyrus, which is still found in the Upper Nile, though it is no longer seen in Egypt itself. As it grows wild on the Upper Nile, it would appear as if the Egyptians had brought it with them from that region, not indeed in the first instance for making paper. For the papyrus can be put to many uses: the lower part of the stem is of a fleshy nature, and edible;

THE PAPYRUS: VINE CULTURE

while the long and flexible stalks may be used for basket-work, and even for making small boats. We can understand why the Egyptians took with them so useful a plant; they would have learned to know and utilise it during their stay in the South, on their way from Arabia.

During the Thinite epoch mention is already made of the vine and of wine. Whence did the Egyptians bring it? Apparently from Asia, for we know the names of several esteemed vintages, offered to the gods in the temples, and these vintages all came from the Delta. We must, then, allow that the vine was brought into the country during a later immigration than that of the Horites, and that it came from Asia by the Delta.

If now we pass from agriculture to industry, we find even in the oldest period the use of ivory, which of course is an African product. As for the precious stones, such as amethyst and carnelian, they were certainly obtained in the country itself: in fact, in the tombs of the Old Empire, so rich and instructive, we find nothing that is not entirely indigenous, and that we may not regard as the normal development of a culture which, though still rudimentary at the Thinite epoch, received at a later time a sudden expansion and growth from some cause which we cannot yet explain.

But the element which ought to exhibit the clearest traces of foreign influence is the script or mode of writing. Now, as we have seen, it is precisely in this region that we find Egyptian characteristics most pronounced. Evidently it was with picture-writing a start was made. All the signs that we meet with from the most remote times are exclusively Egyptian: they are representations of the objects of everyday life. The Egyptians sculptured them just as they saw them, often indeed with a childish and awkward hand, but at the same time in a way that makes it impossible for us to discern in their work a reminiscence of anything they had seen elsewhere. It follows, then, from this analysis that the Egyptian civilisation, as a whole, had its

[Photo by Translator.

birth in the Nile valley, from the time that the Horites settled below the First Cataract.

There is, however, one feature of this civilisation which was undoubtedly brought in by the invaders, and which must have come from without,—I mean the working of metals. Egypt is a country too poor in minerals to allow its inhabitants to have formed the idea of using, and consequently of working, metals. The Ptolemaic legend to which I have already alluded as a narrative of the conquest of Egypt by Horus, tells us that some of his companions were blacksmiths, whom he settled in different parts of the country. There is here perhaps an echo, as M. Maspero concludes, of an irruption of tribes into Egypt who had amongst them a caste of blacksmiths. These blacksmiths could, as circumstances required, work other things besides metal, but what they chiefly made was weapons, and this fact agrees with the warlike character of Horus, the god whose companions or escort these men were.

A people skilled in metals is certainly

superior to a primitive race using only flint implements, even though the latter may have attained a certain facility in arts familiar to them, such as pottery-making or even the fabrication of stone vases. The Horites would seem to have been more capable of development than the native Africans; they knew better how to avail themselves of the resources which the country afforded. Yet we can well understand that the man who can work in metals exercises his power only to fashion some instrument he requires. A familiar proverb has it that necessity is the mother of invention; and necessity also lies at the root of all civilisation. Man was led to fashion instruments because his hand seemed to demand assistance, a something to help him in his work, which at the first was wholly given up to getting the means of livelihood. We may confidently assert that the working of metals had for its first motive this assistance in the cultivation of the soil, which is another way of saying that in order of time agriculture comes first. There is, then, nothing surprising in the fact that when the Horites arrived in the Nile valley, so splendid in its fertility, they should at once set to work to profit by all the wealth offered them by the country in which they had settled. They very well knew how to assimilate what they found in the native population, who were, however, far from being savages. And from the mixture of these two elements emerged the Egypt that we know; and while we admire her brilliant qualities, they cannot, however, make us blind to certain defects or imperfections which surprise us. We are accustomed to call these imperfections conventions. I think we ought to interpret them quite otherwise: they spring from what was always lacking in the Egyptians—the idea of progress, the necessity of doing better, and consequently of leaving their childish efforts behind. Nothing in Egypt ever falls into desuetude: once a thing was found to answer a certain end, what was the good of looking for anything better? why not keep it to serve the same purpose again?

The conquerors, as we have seen, were the followers of the god Horus, and this leads us to speak of what we know of the religion, either of the Thinite epoch, or of the preceding one. In the representations which the pottery has preserved for us of the condition of the prehistoric population, the only thing that suggest itself to our minds as a religious element at all is the ensigns or standards surmounting one of the towers or huts which guard the enclosures where this primitive people dwelt. These standards consist of a kind of perch or pole, at the top of which is placed the distinctive sign of the tribe. This sign is not always recognisable, but sometimes we can distinguish a plant, or an animal such as an elephant, or an animal with horns. It would seem that these ensigns were of the nature of a rallying point, a constitutive element, or, to use a word much in vogue nowadays, the totem of the tribe. Was it already a divinity? Did the people take the totem for a god? Was it the object of a cult, however elementary we may conceive it to have been? To these questions we cannot yet give an answer.

The case is quite different with the companions of Horus, or the conquering foreigners, whom I have styled by the name of Horites. Horus the falcon is really their god, a deity in very truth to whom a cult was paid of which we know little, but of which we can make out certain ceremonies. There is one feature, however, which reminds us of the primitive state of things: the falcon, like other animals, often appears on a standard. If Horus the falcon is the outstanding god of these conquerors, he does not reign alone; there are others besides, both gods and goddesses, especially Set or Sit, a quadruped which we cannot yet exactly identify. Some would see in him the okapi, or a greyhound; at any rate, he is the god of another clan, also of foreign origin, with whom the Horites are sometimes at war and sometimes at peace. Set may have reigned over a part of the country which the Horites found it difficult to conquer, so difficult indeed that one of the kings made an addition to his name, indicating that he had joined together the two gods, Horus and Set. There are also goddesses, represented by a vulture, by serpents, or by an emblem like that of Neith, which is composed of a shield and two arrows. Of these deities the one we most commonly meet with is Apouatou, or Oupouatou, literally, "he who opens the ways." "To open the ways" means in Egyptian to give access to unexplored regions, to enable one to enter an unknown place: truly a great achievement, a glorious title, of which the sovereigns made frequent boast. Apouatou is a jackal, or rather a dog, as Loret has just pointed out, mounted on a perch or standard—a pole with a cross-bar or crutch at the top. The kings were fond of seeing this divinity borne before them when they went to war, as their visible leader and

ANTHROPOMORPHISM OF THE GODS

guide, to point out the way for them and enable them to overcome every obstacle. This deity is the great god of Abydos in the Thinite epoch; at a later date he will take the name of Osiris.

It is to all these gods, whom we shall find in subsequent ages, that worship will afterwards be given, in an elaborate cult, abounding in ceremonies and holding a large place in the life of the nation; but by that date the deities themselves will have somewhat changed in character. While still preserving some traces of their animal appearance, they will have assumed a human form, if not entirely, at least for the greater part of their being or shape. Horus will become a man, but with a falcon's head; Neith will become a woman, with certain ornaments and distinctive attributes; her emblem of former times, the shield and arrows, will be used only for writing her name. In the Thinite epoch, however, the anthropomorphism of the gods scarcely appears; it shows itself only towards the close of the period; before that, the gods are either animals or emblems, as they are still often seen on their standards. And here a question arises to which it is difficult to give a precise answer: has the animal that serves as a standard for the tribe become the god? or, on the other hand, is it the god that has become the rallying point—the flag—of the tribe? It is not without some hesitation that I venture an answer. The second of these alternatives seems to me to be the more probable one. I believe that the animal, whether falcon, jackal, or snake, appealed forcibly to the imagination of these uncultured races, because, to the primitive man, there was something intensely mysterious about its existence as he saw the creature reproducing itself unceasingly, in a perpetual renewal of its kind. Besides, an animal shows no hesitation; it goes straight to its mark, it knows exactly what it wants and how to procure it. The animal is guided by an unerring instinct which, we can quite understand, would be interpreted as a supernatural thing, a something transcending humanity, and exciting a religious dread which induced men to look on animals as gods. One tribe would thus be distinguished from another by the god to which it rendered worship; the devotees of the falcon would be a clan apart from the devotees of the ibis; each would have its special god for its standard,—all this is a fact common to all ages. I believe, then, that it was the god that became the flag of the tribe, but I repeat that this opinion is only a conjecture on my part.

Before leaving this ancient civilisation I should like to touch on a question which has been the subject of lively discussion in recent years. Did this Egyptian civilisation, which we have shown came partly from without, take its rise in Babylon? Was lower Mesopotamia the mother-country whence issued the culture found on the banks of the Nile? This idea has been recently upheld in Germany by Hommel, in France by de Morgan, to the latter of whom it was suggested by his excavations in Egypt extending over several years. That analogies exist between the two civilisations is incontestable, but the development of each has followed its own course, and along such different paths that we can scarcely suppose that the one is directly derived from the other. I cannot believe that Egypt was Babylon's daughter. On the other hand, we may admit that both came from the same region, namely, Arabia; from it they diverged, and it is this common point of departure that explains the analogies that exist between them.

To sum up: an African population subjugated and civilised by Asiatics who came from Arabia, crossed the Red Sea, invaded the country at the south, and who were not slow to mix with the conquered race,—this is, in short, the sum and substance of recent researches concerning the nature and origin of the Egyptians.

II

BEFORE entering on the study of the religious beliefs of the old Egyptians, let us cast a rapid glance at their modes of burial: because then we shall be able to judge, from the manner in which they treated their dead, what their ideas were concerning the life to come. It is evident that, if their motive was the preservation of the dead body from destruction, they must have believed that the existence of the body was a necessary condition of the life beyond the grave; or perhaps that the preservation of the body assured to the survivors some state of happiness or security. In connection with this we shall be able to show that the Egyptians in historic times had very decided ideas which induced them to mummify their dead—a practice to which they attached vast importance, and which was so firmly fixed in their minds that the custom continued well on into the Christian era, thereby provoking the severe strictures of certain fathers of the Church. The mummy became the hallowed expression for the dead in the land of Egypt, and it seems as if it had never been otherwise.

Well, great was the astonishment of the first explorers when they found that, at the oldest period—call it prehistoric, or primitive, what you will—this was by no means the case. Quite the contrary; the methods of burial appeared to answer to quite a different idea from that which prevailed later. In the cemeteries of the indigenous people who had been subjugated by the victorious foreigners, we find small tombs, rectangular or oval in shape, the corpse lying entire, without a trace of mummification, with the knees bent up against the chest, and the hands clasping the knees or held before the mouth. Sometimes one of the hands holds a plaque of schist, lozenge-shaped, or a rude representation of a fish, a bird, or an animal. This position has been called "embryonic," as if it were in the attitude preparatory to a second birth—the best position for a body about to be born into a new life.

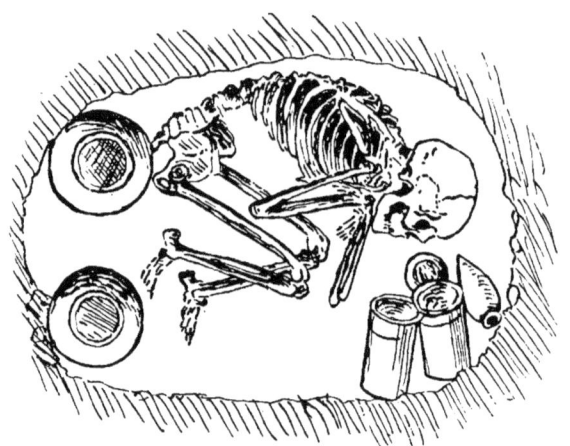

The so-called embryonic posture in burial

But it appears to me that this explanation is a trifle too learned for the people in question. There is another and a simpler one, supplied to us by Herodotus, the father of history. He says (iv. 190), speaking of the Nasamonians, an African people: "They bury their dead in a sitting posture, taking care at the moment when the man expires to place him sitting, and not to let him die lying down on his back." When *we* speak of " men sitting " we naturally think of them as sitting on chairs or some other seat. But in the East people sit on their heels, with their knees up to their breast, and their hands as high as the face. Take a Bedouin or even a fellah,—he never dreams of sitting in any other way; chairs do not form part of the furniture of the establishment of an inhabitant of the desert. Turn over on his side a man seated in this fashion, and you have an exact counterpart of the position of the dead in the primitive cemeteries.

Herodotus also helps us to discover, in the above passage, the meaning we must attach to this custom. This sitting or crouching posture is the posture of everyday life; it is that which the hunter assumes when he returns to his hut or tent, to rest after his labours, or when he eats his frugal meal. Now place beside the dead man—as is almost always the case in these tombs—some jars or vessels containing, it may be, grain or other food, and the tomb will become the picture of the hut where he sat or crouched with his primitive furniture around him. The whole is a rudimentary representation of the life which he hoped to continue after death—a life quite similar to that which he had left behind.

In the case before us, at least, it seems to me that we can very well account for the idea which governed this kind of burial. I am not sure that I can say as much regarding another kind which we often meet with at this remote epoch, namely, the burials in which dismemberment of the body was performed, either immediately after death, or previous to a secondary burial. In certain cases the body was cut in pieces immediately after death, and in others the body was first buried and, when the flesh had decomposed by corruption, the bones were collected and laid in a tomb. Sometimes the attempt was made to give the skeleton the embryonic position;

at other times, the bones were thrown together into a confused heap, whether complete or not, or whether they belonged to the same body or were a mixture of bones belonging to different corpses. This was the case in many instances in the Negadah cemetery, excavated by Petrie, who was even inclined at first to see in these burials the remains of cannibal feasts. I believe that Petrie has in these last years abandoned this hypothesis. The custom of secondary burial is met with among other peoples besides the Egyptians, and it is rather difficult to account for the idea which lies at the root either of dismemberment or of temporary burial which would be final when nothing but bones remained.

Wiedemann explains dismemberment by the wish to compel the *ka* or double to leave the world—the double being a kind of image of an individual, the presence of which was a necessary condition of existence, and which survived after death. With this particular object in view, the deceased was decapitated; and not only was the person himself subjected to this treatment, but even the articles laid beside him in the tomb—vases, ornaments, etc., which were placed beside the body—were shattered and broken. It is undeniable that this is an Egyptian idea of which we find frequent examples in later epochs: they even went so far as to break an ostracon, or a slice of stone, bearing an inscription, in order that the latter, being thus put to death, should follow the deceased into the next world. But does not this explanation somewhat transcend the intellectual plane of the peoples who practised dismemberment? Did they, at that early stage, even possess the idea of the *ka* or double, which lies at the root of the later Egyptian conception of the life beyond the tomb? We cannot say: meantime it is difficult to interpret otherwise this strange custom, unless we see in it a kind of sacrifice made to the gods beyond the grave.

We can more easily understand the case of

secondary burial. It seems to me to have sprung from the desire to disencumber the body of all quickly perishing elements, and to preserve only what endures, especially if the object was to reconstruct the skeleton in a second tomb, and place it in the so-called embryonic position. This would satisfy the same sentiment as mummification—the wish, namely, that the deceased should exist, because he was to continue his life elsewhere.

What happened towards the close of the Thinite epoch to cause the transference of the seat of the royal power from This to Memphis? Was it a fresh invasion from Asia? We are unable to say; but at all events, apart from the extraordinary development of civilisation which distinguishes this epoch, we now witness the definite introduction and establishment, in everything relating to burial, of a method and system completely opposed to all the primitive customs. Dismemberment now gives place to embalmment, to mummification; there is an intense and all-absorbing

A NEW DEPARTURE: MUMMIFICATION

thought how best to preserve the body intact, and to shield it from all possible violation to which it might be exposed, and above all to protect it from corruption and decay. This new departure must not be taken to mean that all remembrance of the old practices had completely vanished; but they were only recalled in order to be detested, and to exhibit the horror felt at everything resembling dismemberment.

In a book with which we shall deal later we see protest after protest unceasingly made against such a prospect, and anything that might bring disaster to the body, and especially against corruption, the most active agent in dismemberment, against whose destructive power they felt they could not take too many precautions. Several of its chapters promise the deceased that his head will not be taken away from him, nor any other part of his body. In chapter cliv.—a very rare chapter in the old recensions,—with the title, "The Chapter of not letting the Body decay in the Netherworld," the description of what the great French orator called "the indescribable something" of dread is painted in the most realistic colours. The prospect of corruption and decay was the most horrible an Egyptian could conceive, and the chapter ends with these words: "I am, I am, I live, I live, I grow, I grow, and when I shall awake in peace, I shall not be destroyed in my bandages. I shall be free of pestilence, my eye will not be corrupted, my skin will not disappear. My ear will not be deaf, my head will not be taken away from my neck, my tongue will not be torn out, my hair will not be cut off, my eyebrows will not be shaven off. No grievous harm shall come upon me, my body is firm, it shall not be destroyed. It shall not perish in this earth for ever." Thus the deceased will not suffer any dismemberment at all, and it is for this that he was embalmed and mummified.

Now, what caused the Egyptians to cling so tenaciously to the idea of the preservation of the body was their belief that its destruction involved the destruction of the immaterial element; it meant the annihilation of the individual, and, in particular, of one of the essential elements of personality, namely, the double that subsisted in the life beyond the tomb. For to the Egyptians human personality was not a unity, but a composition of diverse elements; first the body, then the double, a second copy of the body, not so dense in substance as the material body—a kind of projection of the individual and reproducing him feature for feature, — his "twin," as Nestor l'Hôte called it, or "companion" according to Champollion. During the earthly life the support of the double was the body itself; the embalmed body, however, ceased to exist, and the double, now separated from the body, had to find its support in statues or portraits, which were true representations of the deceased, placed in the tombs. During life, besides, the double, or the *ka* as the Egyptians called it, was so closely identified with the body that the phrase "to thy *ka*" became the equivalent of "to thyself." After death, the *ka* withdrew into the tomb, but it had the power of going in and out. It became the object of worship either by the family of the deceased or by priests specially set apart for the *ka*. It was kept in being by statues of the dead man placed in the tomb; and the better to assure its support and existence, these statues were multiplied. Moreover, a human being could have several doubles: he might have as many as fourteen. The offerings depicted on the walls were of the same nature, being also doubles, ministering to the support and nourishment of the double of the deceased. There was even no necessity for the offerings to be real; it was enough to call them into existence if a passer by the tomb simply recited an invocation to a deity and enumerated the offerings.

Besides the body and the double there was a third element, to which two different names were sometimes given, or it was sometimes subdivided into two elements. This third element was undoubtedly immaterial in nature, what we shall call the Soul. At one time it is symbolised by a bird with a human head; and, according to the characteristics attributed to it, we should rather recognise in it the Will; at another, it is called the Shining One, the Bright One, and then it would be the Intelligence, as symbolised by light and fire. The soul departs into the West, the other world. It can there clothe itself in any form it pleases, including the human form. But these three elements are not severally independent, the double and the soul cannot exist without the body; and yet, in another aspect, the soul has a certain control over the life of the body, being able even to prevent it from dying, if it wishes still to enjoy life. All these doctrines, however, are very vague and ill-defined; here, as in everything relating to the region of ideas or thought among the Egyptians, there is an absolute want of system or logic. Thus we can only present outstanding features. We meet with texts informing us that human personality is divided, not into three, but into four or six parts. We are told of the Shade or Shadow, which, in my opinion, is only another way of naming the double; we also hear of the Heart, which, as among other peoples, is the seat of the moral element. Nothing is clearly defined, except what we know of the nature of the double, round which are grouped all the ideas the Egyptians formed of the life to come.

We now inquire what the prospects were that opened up before the dead at the period of what is called the Old Empire, that is, the age of the pyramid-builders. We have clear enough information on this point in the magnificent tombs of the large cemeteries at Ghizeh, Sakkarah, Dashour, and other places, where something new is discovered every day. These tombs reveal a development in art, painting, and sculpture unsurpassed in later times, and present a striking contrast to the remains of the Thinite period, for which we cannot account. They depict for us the life of a great Egyptian lord, the owner of large estates, with numerous personal servants, and having at his call a crowd of vassals who exercise for his benefit all the known industries and arts of the time. We have thus a complete picture of Egyptian civilisation, in all its details, of what constituted the wealth of the country, and of the luxury with which people in high station loved to surround themselves. As the inscriptions in these tombs always inform us as to the titles and the occupations of the deceased, the temptation at first was to see in these representations, so rich and varied in their character, faithful pictures of how his life had been spent, of the fortune he had at his disposal, of the furnishing of his house and table, of the amusements he indulged in, of the herds of cattle and animals of every kind that pastured in his fields or filled his stables, and of all the workmen who toiled for him. Mariette, who excavated a great number of these tombs, and cleared out several of the more complete and remarkable among them, was himself the first to oppose this idea. He was struck by the fact that no matter what the titles of the dead men were, the representations were always the same; they had no strictly personal character, since we can often see in tomb after tomb the numbers of the herds of cattle repeated in quite an improbable way. Since Mariette's time it is impossible, then, to regard these tomb-paintings of the Old Empire as pictures of the actual life of their owners. They rather show us the deceased transported into an ideal world, moulded on the model of everyday life, in which all Egyptians might share. It is the future life, such as they loved to represent it, and such as they desired to enjoy. It is thus a kind of book, whose scattered chapters were used wherewith to decorate the tombs. With reference to this point, I may be permitted, while adopting Mariette's view, to supplement it by one consideration which has not been taken into account. We have, I believe, in these tombs a striking example of what has been called imitative magic, the idea, namely, that like produces like, and that the representation of a thing calls that thing into existence. All the wealth and splendour in the lap of which we see a deceased person like Ti or Ptahhotep—all the riches, slaves, herds of cattle, estates, all the bands of workmen employed in his service,—all this, it is by no means certain he ever enjoyed in his lifetime. This unheard-of prosperity he never knew in this world: but it was desired for him, his friends wished to assure him of it. It may have been that they considered that it was his just reward; perhaps the affection of his children or relations deemed him worthy of attaining such happiness. To make sure that he would gain it there was no more certain means than to paint or carve on the walls of his tomb the whole environment in which it was desired he should live and move. To accomplish this purpose no great stretch of imagination was required: all the elements of future bliss lay patent to the eyes of all Egyptians alike, in the broad and opulent life around them as it was fashioned by the existing degree of civilisation and by the physical and climatic conditions of the country. Hence we are not surprised at the great resemblance one tomb bears to another.

All the tombs of the Old Empire are on a tolerably uniform plan. To begin with the exterior, there is what is called the Mástaba, generally built on the rock, a massive, heavy structure, rectangular in shape, with four walls almost plain and inclined symmetrically towards a common centre. The building has the appearance of a truncated pyramid, the top of which is a smooth and level platform. On one of the sides is a doorway giving entrance to a room in which a stele is always found—the important feature of the room. This chamber may be the only one, and simple, with no adornment save the stele; or, on the other hand, as in tombs of the fourth and fifth dynasties, there may be several rooms arranged crosswise, or lying in different directions and separated by passages. The roof is sometimes supported by columns or by pillars, and then the walls are covered with the magnificent sculptures of which we have spoken.

Not far from the chamber, and very often on the south side, concealed in the masonry, a sort of recess or cell was built of large stones. This recess, to which the Arabic name of *serdab* has been given, has no communication of any kind with any other part of the mastaba. It contained only the statues of the dead man, of which sometimes there is a pretty large number. Here the double, the *ka* of the dead man, or rather the image or images which ministered to his support, lived; and to enable the *ka* to enjoy the offerings brought by his relatives and friends, or the smoke of the incense they burned, a narrow aperture or passage, connecting the serdab with the room, was formed, and it was by this passage that the double had communication with the outer world.

On the top of the mastaba is the mouth of a rectangular well or shaft of varying depth, from 10 to 100 feet; it has no staircase, but when the descent is made with the help of ropes, we notice at the bottom the entrance of a narrow passage which suddenly widens in all directions into a room, which is the vault or mortuary chamber. This chamber is immediately below the large chamber of the tomb, so that the survivors assembled there would have the deceased, as it were, beneath their feet. The vault is generally destitute of ornament; in a corner was laid the stone sarcophagus previously sealed with great care, and containing a body embalmed in bitumen, but not yet wrapped up in linen bandages as was the custom in later times. Sometimes a head-rest of wood or alabaster was placed beside the body; but in the chamber itself there was no other funerary furniture except two or three large jars meant to hold some liquid, and some

THE STELE IN THE TOMB 71

ox-bones. The body once laid in the sarcophagus, the entrance of the passage was walled up, and the shaft was filled with stones and building chips and rubbish. No one could now penetrate to the dead man's body, which was thus completely protected from violation. Though it was no easy matter to penetrate to the vault, tomb violators and plunderers have left us many a proof of their handiwork and perseverance.

We have said that the most important part of the chamber is the stele. It is a slab of stone, frequently having the form of a false door, and bearing an inscription of varying length, but having always the same general import. It is an invocation to Anubis, the god who is represented under the form of a jackal, and who is closely allied to the "great god" Osiris, considered by Le Page Renouf, an English Egyptologist, as one and the same person under different names. The prayer to Anubis is that the deceased may have a good tomb in the West, and that he may receive offerings in great plenty on certain festival days. Two of these days are consecrated to deities who play a great part in the Egyptian Pantheon, namely, Thoth, the Egyptian Hermes, and Min, Amon the generator. The stele is, on the whole, the only religious item found in an Old Empire tomb; it contains no representations of deities or of worship paid to them. We see occasionally funerary ceremonies for the dead, but no act of adoration or any offering to any divinity whatever. It does not seem as if the dead had any need of gods at all, except those to whom the stele is addressed; and, moreover, as M. Maspero has established, the very invocation itself is conditional: the gods are promised an offering *on condition* that they will obtain for the dead all the offerings in which they themselves share. I will even go further: it seems to me that the request in favour of the deceased for a good burial in the West *does not refer to the tomb* in which the stele stands, since the tomb is already built and finished—but *to an ideal tomb* which he is to have in the West, and which will be the double of the earthly tomb, just as the offerings which he will receive will be the double of those carved on the walls. From this ideal tomb "he will follow the good paths": he will go forth to gain the rich, opulent, and blissful existence depicted on the walls.

We thus see what an important place the double has in the Egyptian conceptions of the future life. This future life of theirs is exactly modelled on what was most attractive in their earthly life. It is bliss entirely terrestrial in kind, in which the religious element is almost as little present as the moral. There is no thought in it of the judgment to which, according to the Book of the Dead, the deceased must submit. And yet it is certain that the deceased becomes a divine being, for worship is paid and offerings made to him as to a real god; his double has priests, which clearly shows that the dead man is something more than a simple mortal. Here we must note that the word for priest properly means "slave," "servant." The double, then, has servants as well as the gods who have the same class of priests—a title which the bilingual inscriptions translate by "prophets." The dead man, or rather his double, having arrived in the next world, is a divine being, the object of special veneration, from whom, however, the living expect nothing. It is not apparent that he exercises the least influence over his descendants. This ancestor-worship, then, is a simple homage to a progenitor or antecedent who is no more, and for whom all kinds of prosperity is desired. The adoration offered is a sort of sequel or continuation of terrestrial life. Ancestors were known and remembered; numerous witnesses were associated with them in the various phases of their existence: now that they are gone from the sight of those in the midst of whom they lived, now that they have left this existence which had a morning and an evening, the supposition is quite natural that, like the sun which reappears after every night, they will return to life again.

If it was the practice in the case of great personages of the Old Empire to depict the life of the future in colours absolutely like those of the present world, it was different where the king was concerned. The sovereign appears to be of a different nature from that of his subjects; he is not of the same race, and he is therefore summoned to another sort of future. The king is buried in a pyramid, and the texts graven on the walls of the funerary chamber are in no way related to those of the tombs of the same epoch. Nothing in these chambers recalls the present, or even the past, life of the sovereign; there is no allusion to a manner of life similar to what he led on earth; only religious texts, fantastically mystical in their nature and often impossible to understand, introducing us all at once into a crowd of gods and goddesses, of beneficent spirits and hostile demons, of serpents and strange animals, with which the Egyptian imagination peopled the region beyond the tomb.

There are few subjects on which so much has been written, and about which so many opinions of the strangest kind have been put forth, as the Pyramids. This arose partly from the fact that the majority of the authors of these books believed that there was only one pyramid, or at the most two, namely, the great pyramids of Ghizeh; and also from the fact, of which they were ignorant, that this mode of sepulture was very popular among the kings of the Old Empire. At the present day we know of more than seventy pyramids, very different in height, it is true, but all built with the same end in view. A pyramid is nothing but a tomb; it is only an artificial eminence intended to conceal a burial chamber. No matter who had it reared, the idea is always the same—the desire to protect the body from possible violation, and preserve it absolutely intact, so that the double might survive in the next world and not be annihilated. A pyramid has, moreover, the same component parts as a mastaba; outside, the temple, chapel, or halls where the people came to render worship to the deceased, and bring offerings to him; next, the long passage corresponding to the well or shaft, leading to the sepulchral vault; and lastly, the sepulchral vault itself situated beneath the mass of the pyramid, wherein lay the stone sarcophagus, which in several instances has survived to the present day. The comparison may even be pushed still further; over the vault opens out a smaller room, connected with the other by a narrow passage; this is the serdab or recess where the statues of the defunct king, which were the support of his double, were placed.

Owing to the great pyramids of Ghizeh being totally devoid of any kind of inscriptions, and of all decoration in the enclosed chambers, it was long believed that all the pyramids were silent, and that they could tell us nothing concerning the fate of those who were laid within them. Mariette himself long maintained this opinion, but some fragments found at Sakkarah having aroused his curiosity, he set immediately to work, the moment he arrived in Egypt in 1880, in the two half-ruined pyramids which had been hitherto neglected. The opening of these two pyramids was his last triumph. Confined to a sick-bed from which he was never to rise, he despatched his friend Brugsch, the German Egyptologist, to inspect the result of the work. On the latter's return he brought back the news that the pyramids were opened up, and that he had found the walls of their chambers covered with religious inscriptions, some portions of which he had copied. This was the last scientific tidings which greeted the ears of the dying man. The news created a great sensation among Egyptologists. It was a revelation, informing the world that at an epoch as remote as the fifth dynasty the religion, I mean the religious beliefs of Egypt, were then very similar to what they were in later times. The principal deities of the Pantheon were already the object of veneration on the part of the Egyptians; the magical formulæ were in existence, and had the same efficacy as was attributed to them later; the same ceremonies, the same offerings were all seen there too. And it was all described in a language whose characters were, in general, quite the same as those of the classic epoch. The Pyramid Texts are a portion of the sacred literature which had already existed for a long time. And this brings us back to the question which we put a little while ago: What had happened between the Thinite epoch and the Memphite epoch which could have produced, not an upheaval or a reversion, but a development so rapid and so stupendous?

Five pyramids have up to the present been opened, and they provide us with religious texts; these go over the same ground, one after the other, but they are not all exactly alike. It is clear that the copies on the walls are extracts from a book or collection quite analogous to the Book of the Dead, describing the destiny of the defunct king after death. The following is the first fragment that was copied and translated, first by Brugsch, then by Lauth, and lastly by M. Maspero, to whom we owe the entire collection and a complete translation of the Pyramid Texts, as yet the only one we possess. What I am about to quote comes from the pyramid of Merenra, a king of the fifth dynasty: " He who stands before his father, he who stands before Osiris Merenra, it is I thy son, I am Horus, I am come to thee, thou art purified, thou art washed, thou art restored to life, I have reunited thy bones, I have recovered what the water carried away, I have reunited what had been severed from thee, for I am Horus, the avenger of his father. I have struck down for thee him who smote thee, and I have avenged thee, my father Osiris Merenra, on him who caused thee pain. I am come to thee as the messenger Horus, he who offers thee perfumes, my father Merenra, on the throne of Ra Toum; thou art the shining guide; go down in the bark of Ra, where the gods love to enter, where they love to go down, and where Ra sails. When it is day, Merenra alights there, for he is Ra. Sit down then upon the throne of Ra, make the gods listen to thy words, for thou art Ra, the child of Nout. Ra is born every day. Merenra is born every day like Ra. Take possession of the heritage of thy father Keb before the nine gods of On, since it has been made ready for thee by the eighteen gods, the very great, who are at the head of the spirits of On. The two gods, the very great, who are at the entrance of the Fields of Aalou, are establishing thee upon the throne of Horus . . . . those who guide thee to their abodes, excellent and pure, which they made for Ra when they set him upon their thrones."

This short fragment, we see, introduces us, at the very start, into the heart of Egyptian doctrines, such as we find, with certain differences, at all periods. In this piece, which is one of the most intelligible, Horus presents himself before Merenra, whom he calls his father Osiris, and recounts what he has done for him. He has performed the rites of purification for him, by means of which Merenra comes to life again; his severed remains, like those of Osiris, come together and reconstitute his body that had been dismembered. It is not the dead king who speaks, as in the Book of the Dead; the address is made to him by a god who declares to him that he has just come to life again, and this god calls himself his son—Horus. Thus, at this early epoch, the Osiris myth is already known, in an embodied shape, if one may so express it; and it already forms the basis of the doctrine concerning the life beyond the grave. Osiris is the son of Nout, the Celestial Ocean, and of Keb, the Earth, and is the husband of Isis, his sister. Beguiled by the deceit of Set, he is slain and cut in pieces; this is the sun descending into the tomb at night; but Horus, the son of Osiris, avenges his father, reconstitutes his body by his magical powers, and places him on the throne of his father Keb.

Sometimes we have variants of the myth.

Horus, for instance, is regarded as the new appearance of Osiris, the form in which he is reborn; but the important thing to emphasise here is the hoary reminiscence in the legend of practices long since abandoned. Osiris is not only put to death, but he is cut into pieces, dismembered by Set; and how does Horus his son avenge his father? By reconstituting his body, by bringing together and rejointing his scattered members. We have here, assuredly, manifest traces of the dismemberment practised in the primitive ages, but now held in abhorrence.

Every dead king had to undergo a fate analogous to that of Osiris. He had to pass through death, he had also to succumb under the blows of a mightier power than himself, whom he could not withstand. But he would also share in the same privileges as Osiris; his son would call him back to life, and procure for his double the needful existence; for this end all the prescribed religious ceremonies would have to be duly celebrated, and then the divine double, safe and sound, would enjoy the life that is the portion of the gods. He would become Osiris himself, and this is why the defunct king is always called the Osiris. As such he will enjoy divine power and intelligence. He will no longer be trammelled by the limits of human nature; he can do whatever he likes; assume all the forms he pleases; allow himself all the joys of earth as well as those of the world beyond; sail in the bark of Ra, the sun in his splendour, —in short, we cannot very well see where the god begins or where he ends, nor what separates him from any other; he will be Ra himself, he will be born like Ra every day, as the fragment just cited says. He can even become a totally different god. The possibilities of the future are for him without bounds, on condition, however, that the magical formulæ, pronounced at the funeral rites, or those put into his mouth, are sufficiently efficacious, and are able to crush all opposition and reduce to impotence all the enemies he

PYRAMID TEXTS FOR KINGS ONLY 85

will have to face. We see that this doctrine is a kind of pantheism very similar to what we shall find in the Book of the Dead. It is, indeed, probable that the same collection from which the Pyramid Texts were drawn became the Book of the Dead, the book that was meant for all alike, for the man of humble rank as well as for the king. It is all the more curious therefore that at this period the Book of the Pyramids seems to have been reserved for the exclusive use of the kings, while the lot of all other deceased persons, even of high rank, should be depicted as a life totally terrestrial in its nature, and devoid of every divine element. Here we have a contrast which we are unable to explain.

Besides what the Pyramid Texts tell us of the lot reserved for the dead, they enlighten us as to the doctrine of the city of Heliopolis, or, as the Egyptians called it, the city of On or An. We shall have to study this doctrine more closely immediately. It amounts to this: Toum, the god who issues from the liquid element, becomes Ra, the solar god, the king who rules over Egypt. Like Toum, Ra is the creator of all things, of his own members, of his son Horus who is born every morning, and who, as we have seen, avenges his father, who had fallen under the attacks of Set. Even at this stage we find in these texts a considerable number of divine beings and genii; for the fertility of invention displayed by the Egyptian mind in the domain of religion and mythology is something incredible.

Returning to the point we left, namely, the dead and the manner in which they were treated, we find at the beginning of the Middle Empire (eleventh to eighteenth dynasty) the custom of embalmment, of mummification becoming general, and taking root definitely. The tomb is the dead man's dwelling, and the walls, if decorated, will show representations not only of the life assigned to him in the next world, but also scenes and episodes taken from his past life, which is supposed to be continued. The inscriptions thus sometimes become biographies; the earthly career and the personality of the deceased come into greater prominence; yet with all that, the religious element is by no means forgotten, as it is in the beautiful tombs of the Old Empire; and texts of the Book of the Dead are carved on the walls or on the sarcophagus.

In the case of the kings of the great dynasties the practice is continued of keeping the recess where the mummy is laid distinct from the large halls or chapels to which their worshippers were admitted. The great temples built on the verge of the Theban Desert, such as Der el-bahri, the Ramesséum, Medinet Habou, are only mortuary chapels or temples associated with their respective tombs hidden away some distance off in the wild valley, to which the Arabs have given the name of Gates of the Kings (Biban el Muluk). I have completely cleared out one of these temples, which was built by a queen whose popular name is Hatasou. On the walls of the terraces of which it is made up you have at first the story of her past life, her miraculous birth—for Amon himself was her father—her education, her coronation by her father Thothmes I., who wished to associate her with him and place her beside him on the throne ; then we have her wars noticed, her expedition to the land of Pount in search of incense, her buildings and the transport of her obelisks. As she was not only of divine origin but a god, she had instituted a cult of herself in certain chambers of the temple, where offerings were also made to her, quite the same as those given to her deceased father. And all this while she was still alive, with a reign of boundless duration before her, according to the promises of the gods. No matter, her funerary cult was already established and would continue after her death. Last year her tomb was discovered, in the wild valley chosen by the kings for their last retreat. At the end of a passage about three hundred yards in length, excavated in the mountain, the discoverers at last penetrated to her funeral chamber; but the mummy had been removed; and on her sarcophagus were engraven only some religious texts, with nothing which recalled her life on earth.

The great kings who succeeded her followed her example. The temple called the Ramesséum, which excites the admiration of travellers, is the mortuary chapel of Rameses II. On it, in the same way, its builder had his victorious campaigns against his eastern foes engraved, in all their details. But his tomb is in the same valley, and the representations found on the walls are simply religious texts taken from a book which the kings affected, the " Book of the Lower Hemisphere," which gives us a description of the sun's course in the different hours of the night. In the case of the tombs of the kings, it is the same as in the Pyramids; there is never a reference in them to their past life, at the most only some names of members of their family.

I have mentioned the " Book of the

Lower Hemisphere." Its title in Egyptian is "The Book of that which is in the Douat." The Douat is the other world, the region the sun traverses after he disappears in the West, and before he rises in the East. This region is bounded by two mountains. As to the locality where the Egyptians placed it, M. Maspero believes that it lay on the same plane as the visible world but beyond any regions known to the Egyptians. It resembled a broad valley hemmed in by mountains, with a large river flowing in the middle of it. Beginning at the west, the valley ran up towards the north, and after making a long bend towards the east it emerged there at the mountain near which the sun rose. I am of opinion, however, that the translation " lower world " is quite correct, for, if we may judge from different expressions which are applied to the Douat, and also from certain representations of it, we must think of it as lying below this world, and of the sun, when he sets, as descending lower than the visible world.

[*To face page* 91.

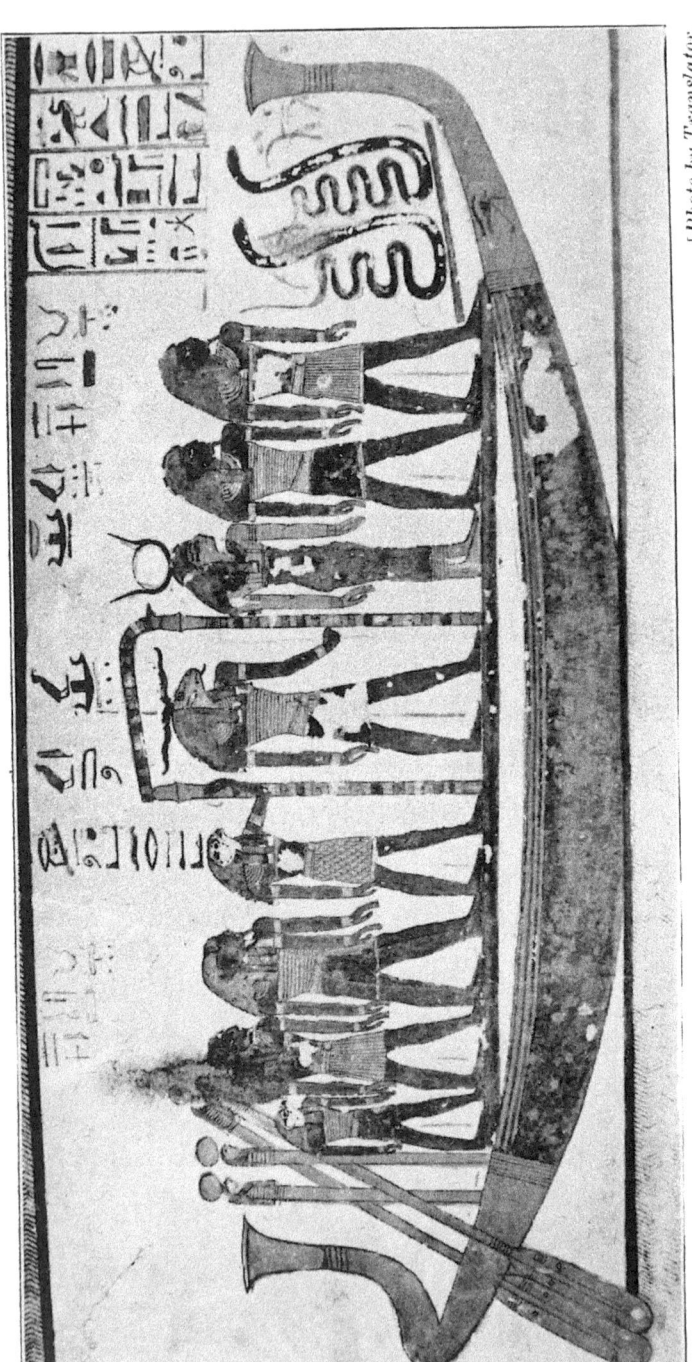

The Sun-God in his Boat at Night.

[*Photo by Translator.*

Each religious centre represented the Douat in a slightly different way, and sought to glorify its local god. The Douat we know best is the Theban one, and the book in which it is described was composed by the priests of Amon,—a work into which they have perhaps imported a certain number of conceptions from other quarters, but in which they above all magnify their own divinity, Amon. Though the sun is not designated by the name of Amon, he is none the less represented in the form of a man with the head of a ram—the animal that is the pre-eminent emblem of Amon. The sun traverses the Douat during the night, and we follow him in his journey hour by hour. At the twelfth hour he arrives at the place where he must come forth to enlighten the world again.

The book is preserved for us in two different forms. At first it was reserved exclusively for the use of the kings, and reproduced with pictures on the walls of their tombs; afterwards an abridged form of it, found in various papyri, was made. It is in the tombs, however, that we find it in its longest form. We are carefully warned that the particular description of each Hour that we find reproduced on the walls or in the papyrus is an exact copy of what is found in the most hidden part of the Douat; we are even sometimes told on which side of the mysterious abode we can see the original of which we are shown the copy.

During the First Hour the sun passes along a kind of vestibule which is 120 stadia in length, called *arrit*.[1] "This *arrit*," the text tells us, "is traversed by this great god as a ram" — for the sun has taken that form. "When he has reached this *arrit*, the dead who follow him do not go up with him: he directs his speech to the gods who are in this *arrit*." Thus, when the sun reaches Ament, the West, he takes the form of a ram, which he keeps during his whole nocturnal course. There is also a distinction made between the

---

[1] The translations (French) which follow are taken from M. Maspero's *Les hypogées royaux de Thèbes*.

dead. The royal defunct, assimilated to Ra, shares in all the privileges of the sun, and makes the same voyage in the boat; but as for the other dead, they do not all share the same fate. Some of them remain in the vestibule of the First Hour, others are ranged at various points that the sun will reach. It is probable that what condemns them to remain thus in a kind of inferior state is the fact that they do not possess the magical formulæ which would enable them either to mount the solar bark or even to be assimilated to the god himself. The gods whom Ra meets in the First Hour, he will encounter later; they form a sort of bodyguard or escort who await his arrival,—dog-headed apes and uræi spitting out flame to light him on his way, and the twelve goddesses who successively take their place on the divine bark. The god thus addresses them: " Open to me your gates, let me come into your courts (*arrits*), give light unto me, make yourselves guides unto me, so that ye be of my members, that I may give you of my body, that I may make you have of my soul, that I may give you of my magic power. . . ." And the gods make answer: "Lo, there they are open to thee, the gates of the secret regions . . . . lo, there they are open to thee, the gates of the other world"

During the Hours that follow, the god traverses different domains. In each of them he has enemies to overcome, and he punishes them by handing them over to cruel gods who inflict the most dreadful punishments on them. On the other hand, he rewards his faithful ones, and allots fields to them which will produce the food they need. This happens during the Second Hour, where we see gods crowned with ears of corn, and others holding palm branches. They are, however, also commanded to fight the enemies of Ra: "O ye whose forms are living," says the god to them, "O ye who utter your magic words, ye who are armed with your swords, and cut in pieces the enemies of Ra (Osiris), ye whose seasons are lasting, and whose years are surely established . . . . dwell in your fields with your barley for bread and cakes. . . . My soul lives as if it were one of you; as you wage the fight for me, and defend me against Apep, you have life through my soul, you draw breath by my body. . . . Cause that I may go on to the horizon and finish my passage to the East. Utter shouts of joy, ye gods of the Douat, for it is I that defend you; utter cries of joy, for I govern your destinies." The difference between the various categories of deities is not very well defined. On the one hand Ra tells these gods that they depend on him and that he is their creator, and on the other hand he asks them to come to his help and defend him against his enemies, and particularly against Apep.

In the Hours from Three to Five the god is on territory belonging to Osiris Sokar, that is, the form of Osiris that was the principal god worshipped at Memphis. The book thus appears, as has been maintained, to be a compilation: the priests of Amon probably collected the different versions of the "Douat," as they were given in several cities of Egypt, and made of them a single book, giving it a beginning and an end. It is in the description of these Hours that we see the fantastic imagination of the Egyptians displayed. Here we meet with genii, male and female; some have birds' heads and are armed with knives; others are monster serpents, sometimes with two or three heads apiece, or they are equipped with large wings and stand on human legs. One of these serpents has on his back no fewer than fourteen human heads, along with discs and stars. All these creatures are far from being harmless. Here, for example, is what is said of one of them belonging to the Third Hour: "Those who are in this picture and who are in the dwelling of Dad (Osiris), they worship this great god, and when this great god speaks to them they live, for when he addresses them he grants them their heart, and they receive their heads at the same time as his discourse. Their work lies in the

Ament (West); it is to cut and hack souls in pieces, to imprison shades, to drag away to their place of annihilation whoever falls under their hand; they dart forth flames, they bring forth fires, and the enemies are beheaded by their swords. They shout and utter howlings of pain when this great god leaves them behind him."

It is in the thick of creatures like these that Ra makes his voyage. They are the soldiers of Ra and of Osiris; they fight the enemies of these gods while they watch over the celestial waters; they are the mysterious souls to whom Ra addresses these words: "O ye whose souls I have made mysterious, whose souls I have hidden, whom I have sent in the train of Osiris to defend him, to escort his images, to annihilate those who assail him . . . . ye whose forms are enduring, whose existence is assured by rites, ye who breathe the air with your nostrils, who see with your faces, who wear veils on your heads . . . . who have returns of offerings given to you on earth by means of the priests of the god . . . . ye whose souls are not overthrown at all, whose bodies are not overwhelmed, open your circles and keep to your places, for I am come to see my bodies, to look at my images which are in the other world; and you have summoned me to allow me to bring them my help, so that I guide by the oar thy soul to the sky, O Osiris, thy soul to earth . . . . I mount on earth and day is behind me; I traverse the night and my soul is united to your forms during the day; I perform by night the rites which are needful for you; I have created your souls for myself so that they are behind me, and what I have done for them prevents you from falling into the place of annihilation."

The nome or domain of the Fifth Hour is the heart of Sokar's territory. The god dwells here in a kind of cell, of an elliptical shape, surrounded by sand and guarded by sphinxes. Sokar himself is very complex in form: he is made up of a huge serpent with two human heads on the right side and a single one on the left; he has two wings, between which a hawk-headed god stands erect. The whole figure, the text informs us, makes but one god. In this Hour we see also nine hatchets stuck in the ground, the first carrying a white crown and the last a red crown—evidently an Ennead of gods. Before them are the guardians of the "pool of the immersed" —five gods with human bodies and animals' heads. The pool is shown in the sculptures, and the immersed are genii with their heads blazing and their bodies in the water.

We will not follow Ra through his Ulysses-voyage in the Twelve Hours of the night, in which, while the figures change, the speeches made by Ra or the gods amongst whom he moves are so monotonous that only Egyptian priests could stand them. At the Twelfth Hour the sun is reborn in the shape of a scarabæus. For this purpose he is towed along by twelve women, and enters in at the tail of an enormous serpent called "the life of the gods," and comes out again at its mouth.

In this way he gets to the east side of the sky, where he is born of the goddess Nout. He is not alone when he enters into the serpent, for with him are his devotees: "they enter, faithful souls, into this mysterious image of the serpent, and they issue from it as rejuvenated servants or forms of Ra every day." They are the dead who have won the right of mounting on the bark of Ra, by having exactly fulfilled all the magic requirements: "they are born on earth every day after the great god, the sun, is born in the east of the sky." This is one of the rare passages which mentions any dead persons other than the king, for he is assimilated to Ra from the outset. Still, we do not very well see how these dead persons arrive at the Twelfth Hour of the night from the earth, where they have been all day, to join Ra just before he is reborn; nor can we discover whether it is open to everyone to aspire to the privilege of journeying through the great serpent, and of coming forth rejuvenated.

THE SERPENT, "LIFE OF THE GODS" 101

"The Book of that which is in the Douat' is one of the best examples of the incoherencies which reign in the religious ideas of the old Egyptians. It would, indeed, be difficult to disentangle from the midst of the fantastic scenes which pass before our eyes any unity of conception, beyond the fact that the subject is the course of the sun during the night, or rather of the king who has become that great god. If we would look for a key to the fantastic symbolism of the book, we should continually run against contradictions, and against conceptions which are in complete antagonism to one another. I believe that we are no more called on to try to reconcile these contradictions than were the old Egyptians themselves.

Leaving the corridors and passages where this book which we have tried to analyse is engraved, we come to the mortuary chamber, where there is almost always a collection of furniture, presents, and offerings, placed there for the purpose of enabling the *ka*, on coming out of the sarcophagus, to allow himself some recreation. Little figures, called *ushabti*, were also placed there, with a twofold purpose: they assisted the deceased in the labours he was called on to do in the Elysian fields, and they also enlivened his solitude. The dead dreaded being alone: an idea not peculiar to Egypt, for it is found also in Greece. This is what prompted the survivors to place in the tombs all kinds of figures which may be picked up to-day in the cemeteries of Egypt as well as in those of the Greek islands or Tanagra.

The conclusion we draw from this rapid survey of Egyptian burial in the different ages is that, in the conception of the dwellers on the Nile banks, life was prolonged by means of the double—that projection, or kind of shade of the body which was necessary to its life, and which continued to exist beyond the grave, on condition, however, that the body was preserved from destruction. This is the reason why the Egyptians regarded the embalmment of their dead as an imperative duty ; and so successfully and skilfully was the work performed that mummies several thousands of years old survive to-day to bear witness to the perfection of the art.

III

THE question, Is there an Egyptian religion? is one which we must ask ourselves before entering on the study of the beliefs which lie at the root of the cult and all the ceremonies depicted for us on the monuments. If we understand by religion a body of clearly defined doctrines — at least in their main features—to which universal adherence was given; or a system well co-ordinated in all its parts, without inherent contradictions, and presenting a harmonious whole,—then we can boldly answer that there is no Egyptian religion. There are beliefs, very diverse in kind and very vigorous in their nature; there are deities, there are myths, and there are cults: but all this nowhere comes before us

THE RELIGION NOT SYSTEMATIC 105

with the same sort of unity which presents itself to our minds as when, for example, we speak of the Christian, or the Mussulman, religion.

For this state of things there are many causes which we must notice here. And first, to revert for a moment to the origins, we see a certain number of tribes or clans, each with its god or standard, all of whom Menes brought together under his sceptre when he made of them a single kingdom. But when he succeeded in subjugating these tribes— perhaps more or less nomad before his day,— and compelled them to settle in the different localities which became their respective abodes, and which formed what were subsequently called nomes or provinces, he did not reduce their particular cults and beliefs to the same level, nor force the tribes to adopt his god, whatever its name was. The result was that each tribe continued to revere and worship its own particular god. The deity which, at the beginning, was the standard of the tribe became the great god of the province; and this great god bore a different name from that of the neighbouring province, and was represented by another symbol.

Side by side with this fact, and in spite of this diversity of origin, there was one circumstance which, if anything, was bound to force the Egyptians into a kind of unity; and that was the absolutely identical physical and climatic conditions under which all the people, from one end of the kingdom to the other, lived. Take any other country, Italy or Greece for example: the lowlander does not live exactly like the highlander, or like the dweller on the seaboard. What determines manners and customs is, in one case, the pasturage, the snow that covers the mountain, the woods that clothe the slopes; in another, it is the seasons that are favourable for tillage and sowing and reaping; in still another case, it is the winds and the state of the sea. But in Egypt, from Aswan down to the shores of the Mediterranean, the conditions were absolutely identical. There was no means of livelihood on its entirely barren mountains; life was only possible in the valley, and there only wherever the fertilising water of the Nile came. The great stream was the absolute monarch of the country, who by his overspreading flood bestowed what the land required: Egypt was the gift of his bounty. Yet the soil could not bring forth except by favour of the sun, the other king who ruled humanity. These natural phenomena, at once so simple and so few in number, struck the imagination of the primitive peoples, who instinctively referred them to their gods; but as these gods were not the same in different districts, there were differences in the way in which the phenomena were referred to their action; in particular, the names of the different gods were kept distinct.

If, however, we study the real nature of the deities whose cult was established in the principal cities of Egypt, we shall see that what distinguishes the different gods from one another is, above all, the name and the appearance with which they were invested in any particular locality: at Thebes, Amon

[Photo. by Translator
The Horus of Edfou

was the ram; at Denderah, Hathor was a goddess; at Hermopolis, Thoth was an ibis; at Edfou, Horus was a falcon; but, in the main, they all have the same fundamental attributes, because they are all the same powers of nature; or, to use a better phrase—for we must here avoid abstract terms—they are all living beings whose action is seen in the same natural phenomena. As Cousin says: "Every infant philosophy is a philosophy of nature, and has already a leaning to pantheism." This expression is absolutely true as applied to the Egyptian religion. It is a religion of nature; the manifestations of the powers of nature under all their forms, or, to use the Egyptian expression, "all the births which are the gods"; anything may become god at a given moment. But this conception has nothing fixed or determinate about it; there is, I repeat, no system at all, no strict logic at the root of this philosophy. These ideas occurred to the mind of some thinker, perhaps, in the far-back past; they go on surviving, and no one ventures to deny their right to live, and so they coexist alongside of others which seem to be their complete negation. Hence, frequently, the most flagrant contradictions are found between one text and another. Add to that, the tendency of the Egyptian mind to conserve everything it had ever conceived, and we can understand how the realm of the religious beliefs becomes at first sight an inextricable maze.

We thus find in the religion a tendency entirely analogous to what we meet with in other domains, as, for example, in those of language and art. Examine the painting and the figures found in the tombs of the finest period. Side by side with a surprising boldness and firmness of treatment, and with an extraordinary cleverness in representing by two or three strokes the characteristics of a figure or an animal, we are confronted with huge mistakes quite intolerable to us, let alone a Greek artist, even though he were not one of the great masters. For instance, you find a head in profile with a front view of the body, or a presentation of the shoulders which violates the elementary laws of anatomy in the most outrageous manner.

That was the way in which their art began; it was the production of mere childhood, and an artist even of the fine period was not afraid of having recourse to its methods; no one forbade it; and so the inflexible law of progress, which fascinated the Greek artists, did not exist for him.

It is the same with the religion; there is no fixed or defined doctrine, and consequently there is no heresy. The gods themselves allow this diversity: Amon will not take it amiss to have other divinities placed beside him in the sculptures of his temple; on the contrary, he will receive them graciously, and will even give them a share of the offerings brought to him by his devotees.

We may, however, say of certain deities that they were acknowledged throughout all Egypt. These were the personifications of the cosmic elements: Ra, of the Sun; Hapi, of the Nile; Osiris often also as the Nile; and Hathor, in whom the Earth sometimes may be recognised. But if we closely study any one local divinity we shall find that the same epithets are applied to him as to one of the great cosmic gods, and that he also may be regarded as the personification of one of these elements.

There is, however, one locality of Egypt where the attempt was made to reach a kind of unity of belief, and even to make it prevail over all the land, and that was Heliopolis, called An or On in Egyptian. That city was certainly one of the oldest in Egypt, and became a kind of religious capital of the country. Its college of priests was very powerful, besides being very learned, and had for a long time a well-deserved reputation, instruction being given in all that pertained to religion, of which medicine formed a part. Later, however, in Roman times, both city and college had completely fallen into decay. Strabo speaks of the place with much contempt. He tells us that he saw there the houses of the priests, who in other days were philosophers and astronomers, but in his time were only engaged in offering the sacrifices and showing the temple to visitors, like one Chairemon, who came to Heliopolis with Ælius Gallus, pretending to great knowledge, but who was generally ridiculed as a blusterer and a fool.

Heliopolis plays a great part in the religious inscriptions, and also holds an important place in the mythological geography, which is by no means the same as the terrestrial, for there is also a mythological Egypt with its cities and sanctuaries. Of this celestial country On is the capital, the outstanding city. It is consequently a mistake if we always interpret a geographical name occurring in a religious text in the sense that it bears in a terrestrial map of the country. We often find, for instance, Osiris named as being the god of Dadou, the city of Busiris in the Delta; and it is thence inferred that Osiris was a divinity of Lower Egypt. But if we consult the Book of the Dead we shall see that Dadou does not at all answer to a city in the Delta, but to a region in the East where Osiris is to be born and receive the breath of life, and where he is represented as the rising sun. Elsewhere Dadou is equivalent to the East, as Abydos is to the West. At a given time the cult of these great gods was localised in this or that district; a local habitation was assigned to them to which was given the name of one of the regions in which, according to legend, they dwelt; and afterwards it was the custom to regard them as native to that particular place. There are several instances of this. What happened in the case of Osiris happened to the goddess Neith. She is certainly one of the deities whom the Horites imported with them, since she is sometimes called "she who shows the way." She was settled at Saïs in the Delta, and her cult established there. During the last dynasties Saïs became a city of great importance, and magnificent temples were built in honour of the goddess; but we must not regard Saïs as her place of origin; she did not go upstream to meet the Horites of the

Thinite epoch, her course lay rather in the opposite direction.

It is interesting to inquire how Heliopolis came to be the religious capital of Egypt. Its name of An or On is, as we have already remarked, the same as that of the Anou whom we believe to be the autochthonous or indigenous population, and with whom the conquering foreigners came to be amalgamated. An means also a pillar or column of stone, and An would then be the city of the column. That may arise from the fact that in that city the god Ra Toum was worshipped under the form of a pyramid or an obelisk. Be that as it may, it is curious that On, which in its origin appears to be connected with the indigenous element of the population, should become the sole city of Egypt which exercised a certain predominant power in everything relating to religion.

The body or totality of the gods of Heliopolis constituted an Ennead or company of Nine (Paut). Why the number nine? We must see here a special idea as to the nature and influence of numbers. If three was considered as the symbol of what was complete, from which nothing was wanting, much more would three times three, nine, be so: it represented a something perfect, a rounded whole, an irreproachable circle, like a certain cake (Paut) to which this name was given. We do not mean to say that the Ennead was always made up in the same way. The oldest list of the Nine that we find in the Pyramid Texts is thus given: "O you, the great Nine of the gods which is in Heliopolis, Toum, Shu, Tafnout, Keb, Nout, Osiris, Isis, Set, Nephthys, children of Toum, his heart expands over your births, in your name of the Nine." There is here an untranslatable play on the words "expand" and "nine." This list is repeated absolutely the same in the ritual of Abydos, with reference to the gift of the collar or necklace, in a text, therefore, nearly two thousand years later than the first list. It will be noticed that in both lists the name of Horus is entirely want-

THE NINE GODS OF HELIOPOLIS 117

ing. The eight gods succeeding Toum are called his children, but he himself is included in the Nine. In the Pyramid Texts will be found other instances in which the gods are ten, eleven, or even twelve in number, because one or other has been duplicated, or mentioned under two different natures. In a chapter of the Book of the Dead the gods are Nine, including Toum; the majority of the versions replace Set by Horus, while some mention Hathor instead of Nephthys. Lastly, in a book of which we shall speak later, and which is found at the entrance of almost all the tombs of the kings, the list is as follows:—Toum, Khepera (Ra the beetle), Shu, Tafnout, Keb, Nout, Isis, Nephthys, and Nou. Here it is Osiris that is absent; he is replaced by Nou, the liquid element.

Let us now try to give some account of the meaning the theologians of Heliopolis attached to this Ennead. At the outset we are struck by the fact that we are dealing in the first place with cosmic gods—with a very summary description of the creation of things. In the beginning is Nou, the primordial water, the liquid element, from which emerges Toum, the sun, the active agent who will create and organise the world. But Toum has another name, Ra, the first king of gods and men. The Pyramid Texts invariably style the god Ra Toum, but the single name Ra finally triumphed. Ra is the outstanding god, over all the other gods of Egypt, acquiring such a pre-eminence that the name of Toum was at last specially applied to the setting sun. The rising sun is Ra Khepera, Ra the beetle, he who comes forth from his own substance— that is, who is born from himself. Although the form of the god with the name of Ra very speedily eclipsed Toum, the latter is nevertheless the older god. He it was who was alone in the Nou, emerging from the Nou, and connected with it so closely, indeed, that he may be almost confounded with the Nou itself. Here we may note that Toum is in general represented under human form only:

THE CREATOR HUMAN IN FORM 119

thus the primordial creative agent has a man's form. This does not imply that he was considered as having been a man, but simply that all the gods, all those creative beings, all who bring forth life or organise existence, all those who assist in giving the world the appearance it has, are not abstract beings, but living beings, to which a form, it may be several forms, have to be given, according to the time when their activity is put forth. Other gods besides Toum would get the human form, but he is the first to possess it immediately after he emerged from the water.

The gods who come after Toum in the list are represented as his children. M. Maspero, starting from this idea, has reconstructed a complete genealogical descent for these gods. They were not, he affirms, simply the children of Toum; they represented his entire posterity down to several generations. Thus the children of Toum would be the first pair, Shu and Tafnout, who in their turn were the parents of Keb and Nout; and from these two deities sprang the following two couples, Osiris and Isis, Set and Nephthys. Now, notwithstanding the great learning with which M. Maspero supports his demonstration, we may ask if he has not been just a little too precise, and given the conceptions of the priests of Heliopolis a more definite and exact form than they themselves gave them. The descent which he constructs does not appear to be established in an invariable way in the texts.

The first pair of children born of Toum, and of Toum alone, is Shu and Tafnout, sometimes called the Twins. Shu, also, is a god with a human form, and often wears a feather on his head: he is called the son of Ra, and even the first-born. He has a special function. He slips in between two other children of Toum, Keb and Nout, when he uplifts Nout, the sky, and separates her from Keb, the earth. This "uplifting of Shu" is the constant expression for the firmament; and the god is often seen portrayed with both arms uplifted, bearing up the goddess Nout, who bends over the earth like an arch. Undoubtedly we must see in Shu the air or atmosphere; in fact, the word for wind is the same. Shu is thus the air which supports the sky. This uplifting of the firmament by the action of Shu is one of the first acts of the creation; prior to that there was only Ra Toum, as we learn from a text from the Book of the Dead, where the deceased says: " I am Toum, when I come forth alone from Nou; I am Ra at his appearance, when he began his reign"; to which the commentator adds, " Ra began to appear as a king when there was not as yet the uplifting of Shu."

Shu became the local god of two cities, Thinis in Middle Egypt and Sebennytos in the Delta. In the temples dedicated to him, he bears a twofold name, Anhour Shu—that is, Shu who carries the upper sky. He is regarded as a warrior god, and is confounded with a form of Horus who is also remarkable for his bellicose character.

Shu's sister is Tafnout. Her name is derived

from a verb which means "to spit"; she is "the spitter." It is natural therefore to see in this goddess the water of the sky, the rain which comes down under the influence of Shu. Tafnout is a lioness-headed goddess; under her name of Tafnout she has no special sanctuary; we know of no city dedicated to her any more than to Shu, but we find Tafnout as a second name of other lioness-headed goddesses, Sekhmet in particular, the companion of Ptah, and then, like all other lioness-headed goddesses, it is not water she represents, but, on the contrary, fire the destroyer, and she then receives the epithet " the burning one, she who lives in the furnace." We thus learn from these two examples that the primitive acceptation of these cosmic deities was speedily divorced from their original nature, and that there is little logic or fixity in the religious conceptions.

A second pair of Toum's children is Keb and Nout. M. Maspero regards them as being born of Shu and Tafnout, but even though a text of a very late period speaks of Keb as the son of Shu, it is otherwise with the goddess Nout, his companion, for she is always called "daughter of Ra." Keb and Nout are rather the two deities whom Shu has separated in uplifting the goddess, who touches the ground with hands and feet, so that her body forms a sort of vault over the earth. We need have no doubt whatever about these two deities; one is the earth, the other is the sky,—the earth being here the masculine element, represented by a man lying on the ground. These spouses have a numerous posterity in the Pantheon. Keb is frequently called the father of the gods; not indeed of all, since several had existed before him, but of other members of the Ennead of Heliopolis. Keb is the oldest father, as Nout is the oldest mother, in the order of the deities. Cosmic Nout is always represented as the goddess sheltering the world by her body, and supported sometimes by the arms of Shu. It is of her the stars are born, and all the denizens of the firmament. Keb and Nout become the parents of the two last pairs of the Ennead: first, Osiris and Isis, then Set and Nephthys.

Osiris is certainly the most interesting of the Egyptian gods; the only one, as we shall see, in whom we discover anything resembling moral character. Here, however, he is a cosmic god, representing an element or a creation; and we have to inquire what his nature in the Ennead is. That he is born of earth and sky, numerous texts testify; but to what idea does his name correspond? Must we not perhaps regard him as the emblem or figure of different beings? We would readily incline to this supposition all the more that such variety or vagueness in the conception of Osiris would well agree with the general tendency which we have already often noted in the religious beliefs. It is certain that Osiris is, at the beginning, the liquid element, the Nile, and this is the reason why he is replaced by Nou in one of the lists of the Ennead. He would thus be "fertilising water," "the water of fecundation," which, united to Isis the vegetative earth—the earth which he helps to enrich by the inundation,—would bestow on Egypt her richness and luxuriant vegetation. In this light then, the earth, which was the masculine element of the couple, Keb and Nout, would become the mother, *par excellence*, according to the title, "Great Mother," often given to Isis.

One of the most common emblems of Osiris is the object whose name is transcribed *dad* or *didou*. It is interpreted in various ways: it has been called a quadruple altar; it has been regarded as a row of four columns of which the capitals only can be seen, one over the other; and M. Maspero considers it as a "tree-trunk out of which started four cross branches cut short near the bole." The texts, however, leave us in no doubt whatever in the matter. The *dad* is a conventional representation of the human skeleton, or the backbone with the ribs attached, and standing on two legs. Not seldom is this skeleton surmounted by a head, sometimes with feathers added, and even furnished with arms and hands. Now, if this skeleton is that of a human being, we may thence conclude that Osiris is a representation of the human male and Isis that of the female. Osiris and Isis would then be the primitive human beings in the cosmogony of Heliopolis, and become the parents of Horus, who, however, does not appear in the old Ennead, as he is of later date. M. Maspero denies that Osiris ever represents the sun; but I may be permitted to point out to my learned colleague that, in one of the vignettes of the Book of the Dead, the *didou* or *dad* emblem stands for the rising sun (chap. xv. where the hymns to Ra at his rising and setting occur), and is there worshipped as such by Isis and Nephthys. Now, if Osiris is the sun, and if at the same time he is the human being that has come forth from the creation, born of Keb and Nout, we are quite naturally led up to the outstanding feature of the Osirian myth, viz., the assimilation between the life of man and the life of the sun: Osiris,

[*To face page* 126

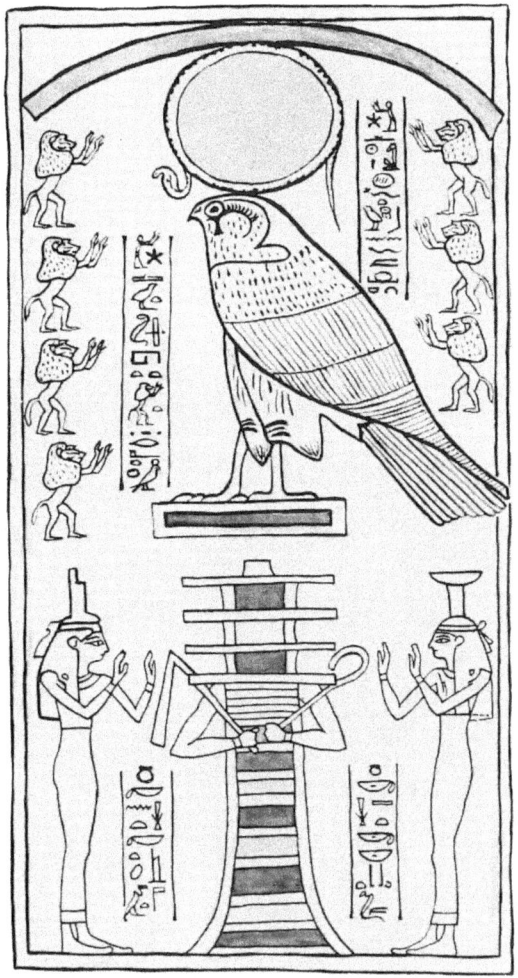

Isis and Nephthys adoring Osiris as the Rising Sun.

(From the *P*apyrus of Hunefer Reproduced by permission of the Trustees of the British Museum)

the sun, disappears; he falls to pieces and perishes, like the human body at death.

The final pair is made up of Set and Nephthys. This couple is often, but not always, at war with Osiris and Isis. I am inclined to think with M. Maspero that Set represents the desert country, rocky, arid, and unproductive. Consequently we may regard it as being in a state of hostility towards the beneficent earth from which Osiris causes rich harvests to be gathered. According to this idea, Nephthys would be assigned to Set as wife, for the sake of symmetry only, and so to give birth to those who will be called his companions. At this point we note that in the theology of Heliopolis the struggle between Osiris and Set scarcely appears. The myths and legends in which Osiris is made to die under the buffetings of Set, or in which Horus wreaks vengeance on Set for the murder of his father, are entirely the results of later developments, and originated in various parts of the country.

Now, does Set represent anything else than the barren desert land, and has he, like Osiris, an astronomical significance? We might think so from reading certain passages of the Book of the Dead; but there is perhaps another resemblance to be found in dealing with this desert god. Just as Osiris represents the primitive human being, it appears to me that we can see in Set the animal world, and especially the wild animal world of the desert that inhabits the land of which Set is the god. Note how frequently it is said in the Book of the Dead that Set himself and his companions assume animal forms: these animals, together with the land where they live, compose the domain, or element, bearing the name of Set, which was also born of earth and sky.

Subsequent legends also inform us that these deities did not exhaust the posterity of Keb and Nout. They had other children besides, malevolent beings, creatures who are sometimes called by the name of rebels; and others still,

HISTORY OF THE CREATION 129

whom the gods found some difficulty in conquering. But here we are getting beyond the Ennead.

If now we gather up chronologically what we have learned from the series of these nine names, we see that from Nou, the primordial liquid element, emerges the sun, the creator, Ra Toum, who of his own body gives birth, first, to Shu and Tafnout, air and moisture; next, to another pair, Keb, the earth in its totality—the earth regarded as the support, the foundation on which all things rest,—and Nout, the sky. The sky assumes its position and begins to form a vault over the earth, only when Shu has uplifted the goddess, and separated her from the ground. Then other gods can be born, the children of Keb and Nout: first, Osiris and Isis, the Nile that makes the earth fruitful and covers it with vegetation, likewise the primordial human pair, to take up their abode on the earth; next come Set and Nephthys, the barren desert land, nothing but stones and rocks, incapable of producing anything, and the animal world found in the desert, with which man has sometimes to fight. We see, then, that the history of the creation which the Ennead of Heliopolis yields is fairly complete. There is but one element wanting, namely, fire. In regard to this point we may ask if we have not let ourselves be rather misled by the etymology of the name "Tafnout," whom we have called "the spitter," as referring to the water of the sky? Ought we not rather to be influenced by her appearance as a lioness-headed goddess, and to remember that goddesses with such heads are generally fire-goddesses? I only advance this idea by way of hypothesis; but, according to it, the two first twins would be air and fire; and thus none of the elements would be wanting from the list.

There is a book extant which gives us the doctrine of Heliopolis in a more developed form than the Ennead. This book is sculptured at the entrance of all the royal tombs, and is called "the adoration of Ra in the Ament, and the adoration of Temt in the Ament." The Ament is the West, the region to which the dead go. The book, then, is the adoration of Ra Toum, for I look on the form Temt as an older form of the name of Toum. There are seventy-five forms of Ra, to each of which the reader makes an address, calling him by name and saying, "Acclamation to thee, power supreme!" and adding a phrase which sums up the chief attribute of the form addressed. Meanwhile, seventy-five porcelain figures, which are the forms of Ra, are laid on the ground. They are, then, only forms or births of Ra; he gives himself all these bodies or appearances in which we discover the different cosmic elements. Moreover, these various forms show that he possesses certain qualities or attributes of which each form is the emblem. Thus, we shall perhaps be surprised to find that one of the first forms of Ra should be that of the beetle (Kheper), but this only amounts to saying that he reproduces himself by himself

—that he is his own son. To call him Kheper (beetle), therefore, is to affirm that he will have no end, since he can be born again unceasingly from his own substance. Another form of Ra is Tonen, one of the names of the earth; he is mentioned in two places: at one time he is said to set his gods over the world and to fashion that which is in him; at another time he is the begetter who destroys his children, thus giving him a certain likeness to Kronos, the Saturn of the Greek mythology. Ra also assumes the form of the great disc, which brings the world to light and which illumines the Ament; he is therefore the sun in his most striking manifestation during the day, and when he shines in the Ament, the West, the region beneath the earth. The moon also appears in the series.

The proof that the book really contains the Heliopolis doctrine is the fact that, among the seventy-five forms of the god, we find the Ennead such as we have described it. The gods follow in order, but the last are not arranged in pairs, as in the lists we have quoted. We have Toum, Khepera, Shu, Tafnout, Keb, Nout: so far the order is the same. Then come two goddesses, Isis and Nephthys, and at the end Horus and Nou, replacing Osiris and Set. The different gods are introduced by formulæ, often vague and difficult to understand. From these formulæ we succeed in determining what elements they represent; but these elements are personified by other forms. We have seen this take place in the case of the earth; it is the same for water and for fire. Mention of the Ennead occurs at the beginning of the book, but we very soon perceive that the book has been composed, or rather divided, into sections, for purposes of ritual. There is no possible order in these seventy-five acclamations of Ra; they are said again and again over the seventy-five figures, which appear to play the same part as the beads on a string; but the telling of them is quite confused; it is a labyrinth where we look in vain for a guiding thread. We pass from earth to sky, from the stars to the abyss, from one element to another, without being able to grasp the means of transition. We can, however, mention some data of great interest, especially if we seek a comparison between the cosmogony of the Egyptians and those of other nations. Thus the attribute of the Word is assigned to the deity. Ra speaks, and, by this means, summons beings into existence. This is one of his fundamental qualities to which the book often alludes. The creative word is one of the most effectual agents of his power; it is also one of his most coveted privileges, which the spirits of the blessed will share when they reach the life to come.

In these seventy-five forms of Ra we do not discern clearly any appearance of either man or beast. It is evident that the beings which owe their existence to one of the forms of Ra are creations of the second degree. Thus, in another text, the dwellers in Egypt are called " a tear of Horus," and one of the forms of Ra is " the weeper," " he who creates the moisture which is in him." What we possess in the book which I called *The Litany of the Sun* when I translated it for the first time, are purely cosmic elements; it represents the world before man had appeared, and that is why we affirm the entire absence of any moral element in the Heliopolis doctrine. Good and evil are as yet things unknown. There are, indeed, enemies of Ra, beings whom he is summoned to fight; but the enmity consists in opposing what he wishes to establish. The creation is often represented as a struggle between the creator and the rebellious elements which he must subjugate. We may choose to see in this war a type of the struggle between good and evil; but, if that be so, the moral value of good is certainly very much weakened. It is not among the cosmic gods that we find the moral law, which is revealed in such a striking way in the Osirian legend.

If we now ask ourselves what name we must give to this doctrine of Heliopolis, we need not hesitate to call it Henotheism, or even Pantheism. All, Everything, is the creation or emanation of Ra Toum, and All must return to him. For the book which we have just rapidly analysed—the enumeration of the seventy-five forms of Ra—is but the introduction to long prayers made by the deceased, expressing the liveliest hope, and the most ardent desire, to be assimilated to Ra and identified with Ra—in fact, to be entirely one with him. Thus the primordial deity, as seen in Ra, embraces all; Ra is the source from which emanate all the gods who are his manifestations, and the dead aspire only to return to him.

This is certainly what we call Pantheism; but I must, however, guard against affirming that the Egyptian religion is pantheism, or even that it began as pantheism. Its pantheistic feature applies only to the Heliopolis doctrine, of the origin of which we are ignorant. Alongside of this very marked tendency towards pantheism we find gods whose individual existence seems well established; and we also find texts in which the personality of the deceased has a distinct subsistence and is not merged in the great All. It is just as we remarked at the outset; there is no single system, with clearly defined lines: striking contradictions exist; and, altogether, we may affirm that the beliefs of the ancient Egyptians present a medley of the most diverse doctrines, in which we must not look for harmony. If we wish to account for them, we must begin by distinguishing periods and localities. This is what we have sought to do for the doctrine of the cosmogony as we find it at Heliopolis, and of that we can say without hesitation that it is pantheism.

If now we pass on to other cities and centres, we shall again find the principle of the Ennead, but not quite so strictly held as in Heliopolis, since in each district it is the local god who is at the head of the Ennead, taking the place of Toum. Thus, at Thebes, the series embraces more than nine gods, because pairs, like Osiris and Isis, count only as one. By way of compensation Amon is there added in as the outstanding god, either of the locality or of the great dynasties native to the place. At Memphis, Ptah is the leading god, and there, too, an Ennead, we believe, may be found; but here again, as at Thebes, it is rather the principle of a triad that prevails—a triad that consists of father, mother, and child.

You may perhaps be surprised that I have not yet spoken of Amon. He, it is true, is the Egyptian god whom we most frequently find in the temple sculptures. He is usually called Amon Ra, which already shows that he is nothing but the great god who is called Ra Toum, or Toum Ra, at Heliopolis. Amon is the deity of Thebes, who comes into special prominence from the time of the eleventh dynasty, when that city became the capital of Egypt on the transference to it of the royal power. After the rise of Thebes to greatness and importance, its god, whom the royal dynasty considered its progenitor, assumed a particularly exalted position among the other

[*To face page* 138.

[*Photo by Translator.*

Thothmes III. worshipping Amon Ra.

Hathor Shrine, discovered by *Professor* Naville, February 1906
(Photographed *in situ*)

deities of the country; and it was in his honour that succeeding generations reared one of the most gigantic temples that man has ever built—a temple that became almost a city in itself, in which we find a summary of the whole history of Egypt.

An Ennead of Thebes may indeed be mentioned, but it is of recent date. It appears to me probable that it was composed for the sake of symmetry with the Heliopolitan one. In the Pyramid Texts, Amon, we find, is hardly mentioned except under the form of Min, who is Amon the Generator. At Thebes he is the head of a triad composed of himself, the goddess Mut, and Khons. Mut means mother; she is represented under the form of a vulture, and may be regarded, in many instances at least, as a symbol of the sky. As for Khons, he is certainly a lunar deity, who duplicates himself, for there are at least two of the name at Thebes. Amon is often called the husband of his mother, which signifies that he specially represents the productive power of generation, like the sun and the water in the world of nature. Like Osiris, Amon is almost always represented as a man holding a sceptre, with a head-dress of two feathers. But he has an animal sacred to him, whose appearance he also assumes, namely, the ram. That is why long avenues of rams, erroneously called sphinxes, often lead up to his temples. The word sphinx denotes a complex animal, a lion with the head of a man, the emblem of Toum, placed at the entrance of his temples, as, for example, at Heliopolis.

The whole doctrine regarding Amon is of a later date than that of Heliopolis, but has at the same time the closest relations with the latter. There are differences, however; some features being peculiar to Thebes, distinguishing Amon from Toum. Thus Amon is styled king of the gods, and this is why the Greeks made Zeus of him. Amon has somewhat more of the human element than Toum, being more anthropomorphic in character; and, as we shall see, he interferes of his own accord in human affairs. He approximates rather to certain of the deities of Greece, without, however, disclosing a moral side in his character, as Osiris does. This intervention of the person of the god in human affairs appears to be a side of the doctrine which the priests of Thebes brought specially into prominence, and to which they attached great importance. Thus the theogamy, or union of Amon with the queen mother, in the parentage of the sovereign, is undoubtedly a Theban invention, like the speaking statues to which we shall allude later, as also the part which Amon plays in the epoch of the great Theban dynasties, when Thebes was in all the splendour of her power, and when her god held the premier place among the numerous deities of the land.

And yet, if we consult all the books which speak of Amon, if we study his true nature, without giving too much weight to this or that detail, we find that Amon resembles Toum or Ra, absolutely ; he has the same attributes, the same power, the same origin. Nor is the groundwork of the doctrine different. We have always the same kind of pantheism, vague enough and subject to what I shall call lapses: at one time, creator and creature, god and man, father and son being kept absolutely distinct; at other times, on the contrary, the one is merged in the other in such a way as to make but a single being.

We possess several hymns to Amon, which inform us exactly as to his nature and the idea which the Egyptians had of him. Here is a fragment of one of these hymns which must be referred to the Theban epoch: "Sole form,[1] producing all things, the one, the sole one who creates all beings. All human beings have come from his eyes, and the gods are born of the word of his mouth. He it is who creates the herbs which feed all cattle and nourishing plants for men; he it is who brings to being the fish of the river and the birds of the air, and gives breath to what is still in the egg;

[1] Translated into French by M. Grebaut.

... he it is who feeds the insects that creep, as well as those that fly, who gives what is necessary to the rats in their holes, and who feeds the insects of all the woods." "Hail to thee, author of all things, the one, the sole one, whose arms are many, who, though he rests, yet watches over men; who, though he rests, yet seeks after the good of all animals, Amon who keeps all things in life. Toum and Harmachis (Hor-akhte) worship thee in all their words, and say to thee: Adoration to thee, for thou dwellest in us; we prostrate ourselves to the ground before thee who hast brought us forth. All animals salute thee, and all regions cause thee to hear their acclamations, in all the height of the sky, in all the width of the earth, and in the depth of the sea. The gods lie down before thy majesty; they exalt the soul of their creator; they are joyful before him who has begotten them. They say: Come in peace, father of the fathers of all the gods, who hast hung aloft the sky, and laid back the earth; thou author of things, creator of beings, prince supreme, chief of the gods, we adore thy soul."

At first sight we might be misled by this hymn into regarding Amon as a creator god, independent of his creatures, and providing for their existence, as the god of the Hebrew monotheism provided. But it is not really so: in other fragments he is called the god of the moon, Ani, or still more frequently the god who traverses the Nou in his barques; and one fragment ends by saying that he has created humanity and all things because he is Toum Khepera. Now, we know who Toum is, the sole, primordial being, who emerges from the liquid element; and we see, therefore, that the identity of this doctrine with that of Heliopolis is complete, at least in its main features.

Another kind of documents which we possess concerning the god are the "Decrees," in which Amon grants to the dead certain advantages and privileges which they will enjoy in the next life. These "Decrees"

"THE DECREES OF AMON" 145

often begin with a sort of hymn in honour of the god. Here are some lines from one of them dating from the twenty-first dynasty: "The august god, the master of all the gods, Amon Ra, the august soul who is as at the beginning, the great god who lives by truth, the god of the first cycle, who has engendered the gods of the other cycles, and by whom all the gods exist, the unique one who made all that exists when the earth began to be at the creation, in mysterious births, in innumerable forms, of which none can know the growth, . . . sovereign lord of being, all that is exists because he is, and when he began to be, there was nothing but he; from the first dawn of the creation he was already the solar disc, prince of splendours and of radiances, he whose appearance gives life to all human beings."[1]

These few lines are enough to help us to understand the spirit which inspires the whole piece.

[1] Translated into French by M. Maspero

Amon is thus, here again, the unique being from whom all emanates, and who manifests himself in his creations, such as the sun and the moon, and is at the same time the primordial water which is the origin of all things.

The pantheistic character of these beliefs is still better seen in a very long hymn, of comparatively late date—as it only goes back to the time of Darius—which is carved on the walls of the temple of the Theban oasis, El Khargeh, and therefore outside of Egypt proper. This temple was dedicated to the triad of Amon Ra; but other deities, Toum and Thoth, for instance, are also found there. Not only does Amon give them hospitality within his sanctuary, but he identifies himself completely with them. Here are some fragments:[1] " He is Ra who exists by himself; his bones are of silver, his skin of gold, his hair of lapis-lazuli, his horns are like emerald. He

---

[1] Translated by Brugsch into German. [Dr Birch also gives an English version in *Records of the Past*, vol. viii. pp. 137–144.—TRANSLATOR.]

is the good god who rests in his own body and gives birth to himself without coming forth from a mother's womb. . . . When he shines on the world the cycles of the gods make adoration before his face, they exalt themselves high as heaven, and they direct their prayers to him, the creator of his children. When he reveals himself in the secret world, they celebrate him as do their companions; . . . they celebrate his royal majesty, their lord who reveals himself in all things, and who has given names to all things, from the mountains even to the rivers. For it is Amon who dwells in all things, this revered god who was from the beginning. It is according to his plans that the earth exists. He is Ptah, the greatest of the gods, he who becomes an aged man, and who renews his youth like a child, in an eternal duration."

We thus see that the god is already called Ra, with the appearance of the king who reigns in Heliopolis, just as we shall find him later in a myth. He is Amon also, that is, the hidden god who dwells in all things, and at the same time the great god of Memphis, Ptah the creator. But the hymn also contains allusions to other gods and to myths of other localities: "Thy dwelling from ancient ages was on the height of Hermopolis, thou traversest the earth and the oasis; when thou wentest forth from the water as the mysterious egg, the goddess Amentit was by thee. Thou didst take thy seat upon the cow, thou didst lay hold of her horns, and thou didst swim in the water of Mehourit, when there was as yet no green thing. Thou didst go to the nome of Cusæ, there thy image is found; it is that of Hershefi the god, thy august ram of Cusæ: and thou restest after tens of thousands and thousands of gods have come out of thee. That which thou didst cast forth became Shu, what thou didst spit out became Tafnout, so that thou didst create the Ennead, at the beginning of being." In several passages he is likened to Osiris: "Thy august ram dwells in Didou, he joins together the four gods of the lands of Mendes." He also, like Osiris, reigns over souls in the lower world. The hymn makes the god travel over the most important districts of Egypt, and everywhere he is said to be the great god of the place: " The heart of the goddess Saosis is glad when thou dwellest in the territory of Heliopolis. Thou art there the water of the inundation and the king of the great palace of On. The land of Memphis opens before thee, in the form of Ptah, the first-born of the gods, he who was at the beginning. Thy throne is set up at Memphis, thy ram is like to that of Amon Ra." We cannot sum up more clearly the Egyptian doctrine than in the following phrase: "Thy throne is reared in every place thou desirest, and when thou willest it, thou dost multiply thy names." There is, then, but a single deity, who bears a different name according to the locality of his abode, that is, wherever his cult is celebrated.

In the great cities of Egypt, like Thebes and Heliopolis, and Memphis too, colleges of priests were constituted, and they became a power in the state, especially if their home was the city which the Pharaoh had chosen as his capital, or where he had sprung from. The lists we find here and there of donations made by the king to the various temples amply attest the importance of these colleges and the influence the priests were sure to exercise in the government of the kingdom. The priestly orders in Egypt certainly held the first rank, and to such an extent is this true that it is exceedingly uncommon to find a highly placed personage that is not attached to the cult of some deity or another. A priest's title might in the majority of cases be only a title *in partibus*, but the holder none the less clung tenaciously to it, for it gave him a more exalted rank, and perhaps secured certain privileges for him. The religion was likewise closely bound up with the government, or, as we should say nowadays, with politics ; and we may therefore ask whether, in the attempt at a religious revolution which Amenhotep IV.,

[Photo by Translator.

a king of the eighteenth dynasty, made, he was impelled to it from a secular or from a religious motive.

The eighteenth dynasty is the dynasty of the great kings of Egypt. It was that dynasty, in particular, which produced Thothmes III., the conqueror and the organiser, the monarch who has a just title to be called Great. One of his successors towards the fourth year of his reign was suddenly possessed by a strange idea. Like his father he was named Amenhotep, and, moved by some influence unknown to us, he resolved to destroy the cult of all the gods of Egypt other than the gods of Heliopolis, and of these latter to assign the first place to the most brilliant manifestation of Ra, namely, the solar disc Aten. This disc becomes his sole god. He has him always represented in the same way, as a sun shooting out beams of light ending in hands. It is to this solar disc he addresses his adorations and makes his offerings, which consist chiefly of fruits and vegetables. Aten is never anthropomorphic, that is, represented as a man—but always as the disc of the sun with rays. In order to establish the new cult more securely, the king changed his own name, calling himself "the splendour of the solar disc (Khu-en-aten)"; and, moreover, had the names of the other Egyptian gods effaced from the monuments, not sparing even his own cartouche or his father's, in both of which Amen occupied the first place. It seems plain that it was against the name of Amon at Thebes that his wrath was excited; and this leads us to believe that his hatred was directed not so much against the *doctrine* or *the god himself* as against the *college of the priests,* who were attached to the service of the god, and whose encroachments he dreaded.

In the same interest he resolved that Thebes should no longer be his capital, and so he proceeded to found a new city in Middle Egypt at a place now called Tell el Amarna, where he set up his new cult, and built a palace of which remains may still be seen. In the neighbouring mountain are the tombs of his family and of the dignitaries of his kingdom; and in these he is depicted in a singular fashion, in a style almost approaching caricature, though his robes and head-dresses are just the same as those of the other kings. His strongly protruding beardless chin, the disproportionate length of his limbs, the fatty development of the whole body, together with a kind of sickly feminine appearance, mark him off from all the other kings of Egypt; and, to please him, not only his whole family, but all his court are seen represented in a similar fashion. This king had certainly a peculiar taste, which has not yet been explained. His capital endured hardly longer than himself; and his direct descendants of the first generation reverted almost immediately to the worship of Amon and the other deities.

The cult of the Aten is absolutely similar to that which was celebrated in honour of the gods whom the king proscribed; but what we have here specially to note is some very beautiful hymns in which the power of the solar disc is extolled. These hymns have always the same theme, more or less developed; they are fragments of the same book. There is certainly much poetry in several of them. Here are some fragments of the longest one:[1]

"Splendid is thy dawning in the horizon of heaven,
O Aten, living god, principle of life;
When thou risest in the horizon of the east,
Thou fillest every land with thy beauty.
Thou art beautiful and great, brilliant, and exalted
    above earth.

Thy beams encompass all lands that thou hast made,
Bestowing life on all creatures.
Thou art the sun, thou bringest them what they need,
Thou sendest forth thy beams upon the earth,
And the day follows thy footsteps.

When thou settest in the western horizon of heaven,
The earth is in night like the dead.
Men sleep in their dwellings,
Their heads are covered,
And no one seeth who is beside him. . . .

[1] Translated into French by M. Bouriant, and by Mr Breasted [and also by Mr Griffith] into English.

HYMN TO THE ATEN

The lion cometh from his den,
And serpents then bite:
The bright heaven is darkened,
And earth lies in silence,
For he that made them has gone down in the west.

In the morning he appeareth again,
Under his form of Aten,
And daylight scatters the darkness,
And all the land rejoiceth.

Then men awake and stand upon their feet,
They bathe their limbs, and clothe themselves,
And lift their hands in adoration,
Because thou lightenest all the land,
And they do the work that is before them.

All the cattle lie down in their pastures;
All trees and plants grow and flourish;
The birds fly out of their nests,
And spread their wings in adoring thy *ka*. . . .
Thy beams go down to the depth of the sea,
And they give life to the child in the mother. . . .

The poet then describes how the god lulleth the child to rest, so that it stops crying; and continues:

"Thou didst make the earth according to thy will,
 When no one was by thee,—
 Men, beasts wild and tame,
 And everything that walketh on the earth,
 And everything that flieth with wings in the air,
 The countries of Syria and Kush and the land of Egypt,
 Thou hast set every one in his place.

 Thou art the one and only god,
 Who hast gathered together all his forms,
 Together with those of the living disc,
 The rising sun, in all his splendour,
 Coming and going, all these forms are in thee,
 O one and only god."

While undoubtedly the pantheistic character is less marked here than in other pieces, because it is addressed to a god who is never seen represented except in one form, yet the basis of the teaching is the same—a single deity who embraces all things and from whom all things proceed, and whose most striking manifestation is the Aten or solar disc.

It was, then, not the doctrine which the king wished to reform. He desired, above everything, to rid himself of the colleges of the priests who stood in his way; and, as a means of effecting his purpose, he sought to unify religious worship throughout the whole country and organise it in his own fashion. He would thus wield an indisputable sway by means of the religion. But this forced unity proved too distasteful to the Egyptian mind, and Amenhotep IV. failed in his enterprise, which was much more a political than a religious revolution.

NOTE

Since the foregoing lecture was delivered, special attention has been drawn to Amenhotep IV. by different discoveries—first by the discovery of a city which he founded in Upper Nubia, and chiefly by the finding of two tombs. One of the latter contained his maternal grandparents, and the other a sarcophagus with a body, which several of my colleagues believe to be the king's own, though it is that of a very young man.

On this occasion we need only refer to the part played by Amenhotep IV. as a reformer. Some would fain see in him a monotheist who alone possessed the secret of rising to the idea of a one and only creator whose providence watches, with loving eye, over all his creatures, even the very humblest. It is impossible for us to adopt this point of view. We still persist in our opinion that the religious revolution of Amenhotep IV. was, above everything else, political in its origin. It is Amon, in an especial degree, whom he persecutes with savage hatred, because the priestly college of the god had become much too powerful, chiefly at Thebes, the metropolis of the cult of Amon. In order to free himself from the priests, he had to abolish the god; and this he set himself to do by destroying the images of the god, and instituting everywhere the Heliopolitan cult of the god Harmachis (Hor-akhte), one of whose manifestations was the Aten, or solar disc. This cult —no doubt less developed in form, but still the same cult—had already been in existence at Thebes, as may be seen on monuments erected by predecessors of Amenhotep IV. What, in our opinion, shipwrecked the work of the reformer was the fact that he found himself in conflict with Thebes, which was by that time a powerful city; and also because he attempted to unify worship throughout the whole country—a thing wholly repugnant to the Egyptian mind.

ARABET EL MADFOUNA, UPPER EGYPT,
12th March 1909.

IV

AFTER Champollion had placed in the hands of the learned world the key to the decipherment of the hieroglyphics, he went to study the monuments in the Turin Museum, and there his attention was arrested by a large papyrus, almost twenty metres long, written in vertical columns of hieroglyphics, along the top of which ran a row of vignettes. He also recovered some fragments, of different lengths, written in hieroglyphics or in hieratic; and seeing that the subject related to the dead and what concerned them in the next world, he called the book *Un Rituel Funéraire*—" A Funerary Ritual." The study of this important document was one of the subjects which attracted Lepsius, then a young man, to

Turin, when he was on his way to Rome in 1836, to join M. de Bunsen, who had been the first to urge him to devote himself to Egyptological studies. Lepsius soon perceived that the title given by Champollion was not correct. The collection is not a ritual, nor does it contain minute prescriptions as to the way in which the ceremonies of worship ought to be practised, or, if such prescriptions are sometimes found, they are only accessories. Besides, the addresses and formulæ used are not pronounced by a priest; they are always put in the mouth of the deceased. Lepsius accordingly gave the composition the name of Todtenbuch, Book of the Dead. This title, however, really gives us no information as to the nature of the book; it only tells us, what is perfectly correct, that it is intended for the dead. The great papyrus of Turin was published by Lepsius in 1842, and his work has been for long the foundation of all the works bearing on this subject. To the same scholar we owe the numbering of the chapters into which the book is divided.

We should make a great mistake if we regarded the Book of the Dead as a work with a beginning and an end, and having its different parts following a logical or regular order. It is not a unity; it is but a collection of pieces entirely independent of each other, something like the Book of Psalms in this respect. The presence of one chapter does not imply the presence in another papyrus of the next chapter. It is rather a collection of prayers or hymns, supposed to be words spoken by the deceased when he has reached the world beyond the tomb. These pieces are of the most diverse kinds, but the whole scene is laid in the Ament, in the region of the West, where the dead man has arrived. In one passage the deceased describes the various transformations which he undergoes; in another, the gates through which he must pass, on certain conditions which are indicated to him by the warder of the gate. Again, the deceased informs us of the malevolent genii he has to fight, or the life he leads in the Elysian fields, in which tilling the ground and sailing on the canals are the chief occupations; in another place he appears as an incomplete being, to whom the head or the heart that is wanting is restored; and here we recognise a vague reminiscence of the dismemberment of old times, as well as a protest against the practice. Again, he passes in judgment before Osiris, in a famous scene to which we shall have to return. The whole is a confused mingling of the most diverse doctrines, and affords us the best picture we can obtain of the religious beliefs of the Egyptians. In the book we are "assisting," so to speak, in everything that may happen to the deceased. But there does not lie before him any well-defined route or path from which he cannot turn aside; the metamorphoses through which he passes, the dangers which he escapes, the appearances which he assumes—all these are not represented as so many successive states which he must pass through, according to a prescribed and immutable law: no, everything that can happen to him—all the possible choices before him—depend solely on whether the formulæ he recites have sufficient efficacy, or whether he is well acquainted with the names he ought to know. But there is no necessity or external law which compels him to pass through these various states, nor are we at all certain that every soul must appear before Osiris in order to be judged by him; there is neither authority nor obligation one way or the other.

And yet this book was indispensable to the dead; it was copied on the walls of their tombs and on the sides of their sarcophagi; it was written on the linen bandages which swathed them, and, above all, on the papyri which were laid within the folds of the body-cloths. As no regular order is followed in the book itself, so these papyri differ much in length and contents. For one deceased person two or three chapters would suffice, clearly those which he or his friends liked the best; for another a much more developed text would be required. One man would be pleased with vignettes or illustrations drawn with ink, like the text itself; another would wish fine pictures in colours, which were often executed at the sacrifice of the correctness of the text. It would be entirely a question of cost as to whether the papyrus would be large or small, beautiful or otherwise.

. The title of the book as commonly given is one with which we do not agree. It is generally rendered "The Book of the Coming Forth by Day or during the Day." A prolonged study of these texts has led me to make a rather different translation: "The Book of the Coming Out *from the Day*," that is, "the deceased's day." The life of a man is his day, with a morning and an evening; and "to come out from his day" does not mean "to quit life" in the sense of losing his existence. We know that several elements go to the making up of a human being and maintain life, particularly his double. "To come out from the day," therefore, is to be delivered from that decreed and determined

BOOK OF "COMING OUT FROM THE DAY"

duration of time pertaining to every earthly life, and to have an existence, with neither beginning nor end, and without limits in time and space. "Coming out from the day" is to be delivered from all these limits. Hence there is frequently added to the phrase "coming out from the day" the complementary expression "under all the forms which the deceased wishes."

The book is divided into chapters, differing greatly in length; in general, a chapter consists of a title, a vignette, and a text, more or less developed, followed sometimes by a rubric indicating at what particular time the chapter is to be read, or what effect the reading will have on the lot of the deceased. The following are specimens of the titles: "The Chapter of coming forth from the day and of living again after being dead," "The Chapter of not doing work in the lower world," "The Chapter of going into and coming out of the lower world," "of preventing the deceased from being eaten by serpents in the lower world," "of repulsing the crocodile that wishes to rob the deceased of his magical power," "of giving breath," "of drinking water," "of opening the mouth," "of giving a heart to the deceased." Then there is the entrance into the Hall of the Truths, where the judgment takes place.

Let it not be supposed that the text is a description of the way in which what is mentioned in the title is done or ought to happen: the titles are the words to be said by the deceased on the required occasion, and their magical virtue ought to produce the desired result indicated by the titles.

The first result to be achieved is that the deceased may become what the Egyptians call *mâ kherou*, which has been for long translated "justified." M. Maspero interprets the words by "just or true of voice"; that is to say, the ability of the deceased to pronounce with a just or true voice the incantations which will give him the mastery over his enemies. I consider this meaning too restricted in its scope. There are grounds for translating the words rather differently. The voice here alluded to is the voice that commands; what the voice utters the dead man thereby causes to live; he thereby makes it a reality, he causes it to become "truth"—in other words, when he addresses his enemies, he possesses the power of immediately putting his commands into force, and from them they cannot escape. I think, then, that the expression "conqueror," the "victorious" or "triumphant one," suits the Egyptian idea better.

Before we begin to examine the contents of the book, let us inquire into its origin. Several of the chapters are attributed to a king of the Old Empire, and even to Ousaphaïs, a Thinite prince, the fifth after Menes. We have, for example, at chapter lxiv., the following rubric: "This chapter was discovered in the foundations of Am Hounnou (a temple of Osiris) by a mason who was building a wall in the time of King Ousaphaïs, the victorious. This composition is secret; it is not to be seen or looked at." Another version (rubric) of the same chapter attributes it to King Mycerinus (Men-Kau-ra) of the sixth dynasty, with one of the Heart Chapters, in these words: "This chapter was found at Eshmoun (Hermopolis) on a plaque of metal of the south, engraven in true lapis lazuli, under the feet of this god (Thoth), in the time of King Mycerinus, victorious; the prince, Hortetef, found it when he was travelling to make the inspection of the temples." Another papyrus, instead of telling us that the text was inlaid with lapis lazuli, says that the writing was the god's own. Other texts, later than those we have cited, also attribute these chapters to Ousaphaïs. It seems then that, on this point, there was a well-established tradition; and it is all the more to be trusted because these statements are made in papyri which came from Thebes, while Ousaphaïs is a Thinite king and Mycerinus a Memphite. It is, then, quite probable that a portion at least of the Book of the Dead goes back to a very remote epoch, to the first Memphite dynasties, if not further back still. Some fragments occur in the Pyramid Texts, and as the doctrine is the same, we may assign the two books to a common origin. It is curious, however, to note that while these Pyramid Texts are reserved exclusively for royal use, at least at the epoch when these piles were reared, the tombs of private persons, executed at the same time, with their beautiful pictures, all relating to mundane life, do not contain a single word of the Book of the Dead, as was the case at a later period.

Some fragments of the Book of the Dead of the time of the Old Empire have been preserved. A few years ago the discovery of tombs of the eleventh and twelfth dynasties supplied us with quite a large number. Chapter xvii. is especially frequent in these fragments: it is one of the most important, carrying us back at once into the very heart of the Heliopolitan cosmogony. Its text is much shorter than it afterwards became; but even at this epoch the meaning of the text was beginning to be lost, as is proved by the glosses and commentaries introduced into it. A sentence is often broken by the question, "What is that?" to which the commentator replies by an explanation.

With the eighteenth dynasty we witness the emergence of texts in great numbers, on papyrus and also on the walls of tombs. These papyri are written in a style of handwriting midway between pure hieroglyphics and the cursive writing erroneously styled hieratic. They are of very unequal length, and generally contain only a selection of the chapters of the book as published by Lepsius. Accordingly, if we wished to reconstruct the whole of the book in conformity with the version of the period, we should have to collate more than twenty-four papyri, and yet we should have not brought together all the chapters current in the Saïte epoch. On the other hand, there are other chapters which were dropped in later times. No order of

THE SAÏTE RECENSION

any kind is found in these papyri: all that we can say is that nearly every one ends with the same chapter, but they all have a different beginning, and the judgment scene, one of the most important, is sometimes found even in two places, one of which is quite at the beginning of the text. Frequently too there is a hymn to Osiris as an introduction.

In the Saïte epoch, that is, towards the seventh century before our era, a revision and a complete codification of the Book of the Dead was made; a definite order was adopted, to which the copyists did not adhere strictly, but only in a general way. Various chapters were added to the text, especially those that appear last in the Turin papyrus, containing fantastic and strange words. We might also say that a text was then settled, from which as little deviation as possible was made. But this work was done by men who had certainly lost the meaning of what they wrote, and a large number of glosses were introduced which usually render the text only the more obscure. Though a comparison of the fidelity of the copies with that of Hebrew MSS. is out of the question, it is certain that the number of variants in the Saïte version is much fewer than in the Theban texts.

Anyone who is familiar with the Book of the Dead is struck at the first glance with the difficulty of translating it—a difficulty of precisely the same nature as we find in the Pyramid Texts. For this there are various reasons. There is first the inaccuracy of the text itself. The copyists who worked for the dead were mere craftsmen, who displayed all the more carelessness in proportion to their very common ignorance of what they were writing. Besides, if the manuscript was not correct, nobody would be prejudiced, no interest would suffer by it: nobody would ever see it again; it would be hidden in the tomb, perhaps even wrapped up in the bandages round the deceased, and no one would ever trouble himself to read it. Next, the question may be asked whether these religious texts, composed a thousand years perhaps before the date when they had to be reproduced, had not become enigmas as insoluble to these unlettered men as they are to us. Many of the words put in the mouths of the defunct are magical words, which would be all the more efficacious the less they were understood. Moreover, there is a considerable number of allusions to mythological facts with which we are only imperfectly acquainted. All this does not help the translator in his task—far from it.

It is not the grammar that is the stumbling-block; it is generally very simple. The meaning of the words, too, is plain, and yet it often happens that a phrase which is easy to translate yields a fantastic idea with quite a childish, not to say a nonsensical, look. We cannot, however, be sure that it struck the old Egyptians in this way. Beneath this strange mode of speech, which at first sight makes us smile, there may lie hidden elementary truths and ideas of the greatest simplicity. We have not discovered them, because we are not yet sufficiently well acquainted with the Egyptian way of expressing abstract ideas. Evidently it was by metaphors, and until we have found the key to them we are compelled to adhere to the literal meaning, which may lead us astray, or leave us in ignorance of the true meaning—the meaning, viz., as clothed in a figurative expression drawn from what strikes the senses or from the material world. Thus the translation of the Book of the Dead, like that of the Book of the Pyramids, is still only provisional in many respects, for, so far, we have only got the general drift of it.

Several of the old papyri begin with a hymn to Osiris, the text of which often varies. Here is one of the most complete. Osiris, a figure in black, is seated in a sanctuary, while the deceased and his wife approach him and address him thus: "Hail, venerable god, great and beneficent prince of eternity, he whose dwelling is in the Sektit bark. He is acclaimed in heaven and on earth; he is exalted by the people of the past and of the present. Great is the fear which he inspires in the hearts of men, of the shining ones, and of the dead. His soul has been given to him at Didou, his strength at Hanes, his image at On, his power over all forms, in the double sanctuary. I am come to thee; my heart contains truth, my heart contains no falsehood; grant me to be among the living, to go up and down the river in thy train." We note here that Osiris is represented as a god that has been reconstituted or reconstructed; and the different elements constituting his personality come from various localities. His chief attribute, according to this text, is to inspire fear, dread; it is in this quality that he was adored, especially at Heracleopolis, a city in Middle Egypt, with which can be associated several features of the Osiris myth.

The chapter that is numbered I. in the Turin text also occupies frequently the same position in the Theban text; indeed, the title mentions that it is called "the day of the burial"; and the vignette illustrating it shows the funeral procession on the way to deposit the mummy in the Western Desert. The deceased speaks to Osiris in these words: "O Bull of the Ament, it is Thoth, the king eternal, who is there. I am the great god in the divine bark. I have fought for thee. I am one of the gods, the powers, who make Osiris triumphant over his enemies, on the day of the weighing of the words (that is, the day of the judgment). I am of thy family, Osiris. I am one of these gods, children of Nout, who slay the enemies of Osiris and who chain up his adversaries in his defence. I am of thy family, Horus; I have battled for thee; I have come forward in thy name. I am Thoth, who makes Osiris victorious over his enemies, on the day of the weighing of words in the house of the prince who is in Heliopolis. I am Didou, son of Didou, conceived at Didou, and born at Didou; Didou is my name. I am with the weeping sisters who make mourning for Osiris at Rekhit, and who make Osiris victorious over his enemies. It is Ra who has commanded Thoth to make Osiris victorious over his enemies: a command carried out by Thoth on my behalf."

So far, the deceased is represented as being himself, or Thoth, or one of the children of Nout, or even Didou—that is, Osiris. Now, however, he goes on to tell us that he is a priest, and that he performs various duties which the cult prescribes: " I am with Horus on the day of the celebration of the festivals of Osiris, when they make great offerings to Ra, on the festival of the sixth day of the month, and on the festival of the seventh day at Heliopolis. I am the priest in Didou, and I magnify him who is on the height. I am the prophet in Abydos, on the day when the earth is raised. I am he who beholdeth the mysteries of Restau. I am he who reciteth the liturgies of the Spirit who is at Didou. I am the *Sem* priest in all that pertaineth to his office." Then comes an invocation: " O ye who guide beneficent souls into the house of Osiris, do ye bring along with you the soul of the deceased into the house of Osiris; let him see as ye see; let him understand as ye understand; let him stand up as ye stand up; let him sit as ye sit, in the house of Osiris. . . . O ye who open the ways and who prepare the paths for beneficent souls in the house of Osiris, open ye the ways and prepare the paths for the soul of the deceased who is with you; let him enter boldly, and go forth in peace, without being opposed and without being repulsed. Let him enter when he pleases, and go forth when he wishes; for he is victorious with you; and let that be done which he will command in the house of Osiris. No transgression has been found in him; the balance is free of everything that concerns him."

In later papyri the following rubric is added to this chapter: "He who knows this book on earth, or on whose coffin it has been written, may come out from the day when he pleases, and again enter his dwelling, without anyone repulsing him. And there shall be given to him bread, beer, much flesh meat, upon the altar-table of Ra; he shall receive allotment of land in the garden of Aalou, and there shall be given to him grain, and he shall grow green (flourish) again, like what he was upon earth."

We now see what sort of efficacy the book had. It is enough if the deceased knew it when he was alive in this world, or if he has it painted on his coffin when he dies, to put him in full possession of the privileges and the blessed life awaiting him in the gardens of Aalou. Such was the magical virtue of the words of the book, whose composition the old Egyptians attributed to Thoth.

The chapter we have discussed gives a fairly correct idea of the book as a whole: there is the same vagueness and indeterminate nature in its teaching. In one place the dead man is Thoth (Hermes)—he who has the power of making Osiris triumphant over his enemies; in another he is Osiris himself, he of Didou, he to whom life comes back again in the East; a little further on, he is only a priest, or even a suppliant, who addresses the souls in the house of Osiris and earnestly entreats them to open the road for him. He comes out of the judgment scathless, since the balance " is free of everything that concerns him." He changes swiftly from one state to another, from possessing the might of Thoth to the condition of the unfortunate deceased begging for pity to be shown to him, and all this without the slightest hint as to the reasons for such sudden and total transformations. The whole appears rather incoherent; but it mattered little to the Egyptian if his ideas clashed with one another; what he dreaded was rules or system.

The myth of Osiris is by this time full-grown, as we see from several allusions. Osiris is a dead man for whom mourning is made; he is avenged by his son Horus, and offerings are made to him. He is spoken of as one whose heart is without movement; besides, he is conceived and born in Didou; mention is also made of the day when words are weighed, or the day of judgment. This will refer to the day when Osiris triumphs over his enemies; probably they will be condemned, when they will receive their death sentence—a sentence which we never see pronounced against the deceased. Thus, Osiris lives; he seems to be, as we have seen in speaking of the Ennead, the primordial man: and he dies. Is it, then, man that is thus likened to the sun which sets and disappears; or, on the contrary, is it the sun which perishes like a human being, after having been seen by the inhabitants of the earth? We may put the question, but I doubt much if the old Egyptians themselves could give us a definite answer.

Close to chapter i. we sometimes find the scene of the weighing of the soul; at other times hymns to the rising and the setting sun are found. These have some affinity with the hymn to the Aten of Amenhotep IV. Next, there is sometimes a well-defined group of passages, that of the Transformations, bearing a general title, "The Beginning of the Transformations of Osiris, to the end that his soul may live and his body be renewed eternally." These Transformations are eleven in number; but the whole of these are not often found together, the first being rather rare: " To take the form of the god which gives light in the darkness "—an evident reference to the moon. Then follow in succession the chapters of the *Bennou* bird, which M. Loret calls the ash-coloured or blue heron; of the soul, which may be either a ram or a bird with a human head; of Ptah, not the god of Memphis, but a cosmic deity born of Keb; of the falcon of gold and the powerful falcon; of the swallow; of the serpent; of the crocodile; and of the lotus. These chapters, which vary much in length, are certainly the relics of a doctrine of metempschyosis or transmigration of souls, which has none of the strictness or sharpness of similar doctrines in other religions. By assuming these forms the dead man hopes to succeed to the attributes or privileges peculiar to each of these creatures. Here, for instance, is what is said of the serpent: "I am the serpent (literally, the son of the ground), whose years are long; I lie down and am born every day; I am the serpent at the ends of the earth; I lie down, then I am born, I am re-established, I grow young again every day."

The description of the garden of Aalou initiates us into the geography of these Elysian fields, where the dead devote themselves chiefly to agricultural pursuits, assisted by the *Answerers* — these little statues which are found sometimes by hundreds in the tombs, carrying the implements of toil. The deceased calls on them to be always ready when he requires them, and the figures reply, "Lo, here I am, whenever thou callest me."

Chapter xvii., one of the most important, opens with the cosmogony of Heliopolis—the birth of Toum coming out of the water, and the uplifting of the firmament. This is certainly a bit of the theology of Heliopolis, like the greater part of the Book of the Dead. Else we might look for a different place of origin—to Abydos, for instance, since everything relating to the myth of Osiris comes from there. Yet undoubtedly it is Heliopolis that is the reputed scene of what I consider to be the heart of the Book of the Dead, the Judgment. This part is also the most interesting of all, because it is almost the only one in which a moral element appears. Up to this point, as we have seen, the gods are deities more or less cosmic; they are divinities whose nature-character is strongly marked, and whose relations with man are precisely the same as those which he holds with natural phenomena. Consequently, the conception of good and evil, and everything connected with conscience, are entirely absent. How comes it, then, that, side by side with such strongly accented pantheistic tendencies, we have a moral code as well, which for loftiness may well be placed beside others which claim our admiration? We are here in presence of a contradiction which is not peculiar to Egypt—a something inherent in the nature of man—

THE JUDGMENT OF THE SOUL

namely, conscience, which always appears again and again, and always will assert itself as the standard of right and wrong. As Osiris stood for the primeval man, he could not be a stranger to those feelings which govern man in relation to his conduct: it is man himself who must be his own judge.

The scene of the Judgment occupies chapter cxxv. of the book. One of the longest, it is also one of the commonest. Indeed, it of all others had the greatest value for the deceased, and summed up the whole book for him. Frequently it follows chapter i., but it is found more often near the end of the book. It consists of three parts, with an introduction bearing different titles, one of which is: " Words said when one approaches the Hall of the Two Truths, or the Two Justices, to the end that one may be delivered from his sins and see the faces of the gods." It is curious that Truth, or, as Renouf renders it, Justice, should be represented by two goddesses, absolutely alike; and one of the texts informs us that one of them is at the East and the other at the West. They keep guard, therefore, over the two extremities of the Hall or Seat of Osiris. We have here a singular mingling of cosmic or nature ideas relative to the course of the Sun, with a scene which is altogether human in its character, and implies, above all, an order of ideas entirely apart from nature. The dead man draws near with his wife; the two have their hands raised in adoration; before entering, he makes his addresses to Osiris, who is in his hall or pavilion, and he says: " Hail to thee, mighty God, Lord of Justice. I come to thee, my Lord, to behold thy beauties; I know thee, I know the name of the two-and-forty gods who are with thee, who devour those who meditate evil, who drink their blood the day when a man gives account of himself before Unnofer. Truly thy name is: He whose two eyes are those of Justice. Behold me, I have come to thee, I bring the truth to thee, and I will put aside all lying." Then he begins a confession which he repeats later when he enters the Hall: "I have not done evil to any man; I am not one of those who put to death his kindred; I am not one who telleth lies in place of truth. . . . I am not a doer of that which the gods abhor; I have not done wrong to a servant in the eyes of his master; I have not caused famine; I have not caused weeping; I am not a murderer; I have not given commands for murder; I have not caused men to suffer; I have not diminished the temple offerings; I have not lessened the bread given to the gods; I have not robbed the dead of their funeral offerings; I am not an adulterer; I have not diminished the grain measure; I have not shortened the palm's length. . . . I have not pressed down the arm of the balance; I have not falsified the tongue [of the balance]; I have not snatched away the milk from the mouth of children; and I have not driven off the cattle from their pastures." Then follow some delinquencies which have a purely Egyptian smack: "I have not stopped the water at its appointed time; I have not diverted a runnel of water in its course." Obviously, water, being in Egypt the producer of life, is regarded with a veneration and respect that it could not have in a country not wholly dependent on a large river and on inundation. There are also trespasses with reference to the gods. We have seen above that the dead man denies that he had diminished or stolen the offerings; other transgressions refer to the ceremonies, like the following, the last in the list: "I have not put myself in the way of the god when he cometh forth," that is, when the god is led forth in procession in the temple at his festival. And at the very end the dead man exclaims: "I am pure, I am pure . . . . let no harm come to me in this land, in the Hall of Justice, because I know the name of all the gods who make their appearance in it."

The foregoing is only a preliminary confession made at the gate; it is not enough to

THE WEIGHING BEFORE OSIRIS 189

justify the deceased. Anubis comes and takes him by the hand, and leads him into the Hall of Justice. At the end of it Osiris, the supreme judge, is enthroned in a pavilion; and sometimes with him are four judges as assessors, the gods of the cardinal points. In front of the judge is a balance, the tongue of which Thoth (in the frontispiece it is Horus) verifies, while round about him are forty-two deities to whom the deceased has referred as being ready to devour the guilty and drink his blood. These gods seem quite fit to inspire him with terror. Sometimes also there is *the* Enemy *par excellence*, "he who eats the dead,"—a monster with a composite body of three animals, a crocodile, a lion, and a hippopotamus. But what completes the chilling terror of the deceased is that he feels his heart is no longer in himself; he sees it before him in one of the scales of the balance, and the goddess of Justice in the other. His first cry is to it: "O Heart of my mother, Heart of my birth, Heart that was mine on earth, rise not up as a witness against me, be not my adversary before the Divine Powers, let not the scale weigh against me in presence of the guardian of the Balance; do not say, '*See there what he has done, in truth he has done it*'; do not suffer wrongs to arise against me in presence of the great god of the Ament." Then he begs his heart to come back to him, and to be joined to him anew. The heart listens to his request, and it is found to be neither too heavy nor too light. Yet, all the same, the deceased must make his defence; and for this purpose he challenges by name each of the forty-two deities who assist in the judgment—the same that are ready to devour him if he is found guilty— and he calls each of them to witness that he has not committed any of the forty-two sins which would entail his condemnation: "O thou who stridest with long steps, and who makest thine appearance in Heliopolis, I am not a doer of wrong. O thou who holdest the fire, and who makest thine appearance in

Kheraha, I have not been a robber. O thou god (Thoth) with the long beak (beak of the ibis), and who appearest in Eshmoun, I am not evil-minded," and so on through the forty-two. He thus repeats in greater detail the confession made at the entrance. When we analyse this confession we are struck with its lofty character and the development of the moral sense that it reveals. If we compare it with the Decalogue, in those commandments, for instance, which govern the relations between man and man, we find that murder, adultery, and theft are forbidden in both codes; false witness-bearing is forbidden also in the Egyptian law under the calumny of "doing wrong to a servant in the eyes of his master"; and if covetousness is not specially named, the Egyptian law, on the other hand, accentuates very forcibly the forbidding of lying and deceit, a prohibition which Egyptians of the present day appear often to forget. Blasphemy is banned, as well as words spoken against the king.

Certain obligations imposed are interesting, like the following: " I have not been deaf to the words of justice (righteousness)." I was saying that covetousness is not specially cited, at least not so clearly as in the Hebrew law, but perhaps it is meant by the sentence which Renouf translates thus: " I have no strong desire but for my own property."

During the confession Thoth is weighing the heart, and afterwards he reports to the judge as to the state of the balance. I translate from a papyrus written for a princess: " The princess is triumphant; she has been weighed in the balance before the guardian Anubis, under the command of the god of Hermopolis himself, in presence of the powers of the Hall of Justice. No fault has been found in her; her heart is according to truth, her members are pure, her whole body is free from evil, the tongue of the balance shows true; there is no doubt; all her members are perfect." Then comes the decree of Osiris, the eternal god: " Let her go forth victorious, to enter into every place she pleases, and be with the spirits and the gods. She will not be repulsed by the guardians of the gates of the West; grant her food, offerings, drinks . . . . and clothes of fine linen ": whereupon her heart is restored to her.

Here, then, we have the Egyptian conception of conscience. Thus the most terrible accuser of man—he who can most effectually bring down on his head the punishment he has earned,—he whose assertions no one has skill to gainsay, is man himself, his own heart, that knows too well that he has broken a hundred times that moral law which he knows perfectly.

When the dead man emerges triumphantly from the Hall of Justice, he goes wherever he wills. Sometimes he enters a hall called " The Great "; he declares that he is the man to whom those who see him say, " Come in peace." Every part of the hall asks him if he knows its name, the door, the floor, etc., and everywhere he is allowed to pass. Later, he goes to see the fourteen abodes, or, as M. Maspero translates the words, "the fourteen islands of the West." In one of these are the two green sycamores between which the sun passes as he rises in the firmament; in another we see the Nile issuing from the caverns of Elephantiné and running as far as Heliopolis, where it was supposed to find a fresh source, for in the Egyptian mythology there are two Niles. It is at this point the Book of the Dead of the Theban period usually ends, with the words, "It is finished." We now leave the dead man in this ill-defined existence of his, in which he is at one time the double of his earthly personality, at another a god, Osiris or Ra himself, at another still, a bird or a lotus—an existence in which he can assume any form he pleases, or contend with malignant spirits, or devote himself to working in the fields of the gardens of Aalou, where he has numberless courses open to him, without following any definite line or complying with any obligation. All this body of ideas, we repeat, represents the conceptions the Egyptian had of the future life, but there is no possibility of discovering in it a systematic or settled doctrine.

We have seen that under the Old Empire the deceased goes joyfully forth to enter on a life beyond the tomb modelled on the lines of the present world, in the lap of wealth and prosperity; at a later period we have that life described for us, in which the human being becomes a god, and may even be called Ra or Osiris, and enjoy all the privileges which fall to the lot of the gods. We have witnessed Osiris not only absolving the deceased, but commanding him to be treated as a god. There was nothing at all in such a future to terrify the deceased. On the contrary, some who were tired of life were fascinated by the brilliant prospects before them, and they clamoured for death with loud cries; but, if I may use the expression, it was for a "correct" or "proper" death, that is, one followed by the due fulfilment of all the religious ceremonies and obsequies agreeable to all the prescriptions and conditions necessary for entering into the joys and pleasures of the West. Finally, it was essential that the various elements which made up the human personality should all agree to the step: the union between them had to be maintained. It might happen, however, that one of them, the soul, would not consent to die. A papyrus preserved in Berlin affords a curious example of this. Unfortunately, nearly the whole of the beginning of it is lost. There we read of an unhappy man who addresses his soul and beseeches it to allow him to die; but the soul at first remains deaf to his prayers. Some words let fall by the poor fellow in his misery, wearied of life, give us an inkling of his condition. He calls himself a gentle, sweet man; he is not of those proud fellows who are always successful; when one day misfortune—it seems to have been a sore disease—overtook him, and he was forsaken of his brethren and friends; no one stood faithfully

DIALOGUE OF A MAN WITH HIS SOUL 197

by him; what he had done yesterday, everybody was in a hurry to forget; and his very name had become loathsome to all.

The unfortunate wretch now opens his mouth and replies to some words spoken by his soul. The conversation takes place in presence of witnesses, but who and how many they were we do not know. He reproaches his soul with having forsaken him in the day of misfortune, and with giving him the wicked counsel of urging him to cast himself into the fire instead of paying him the last rites. She, the soul, ought to have refused to keep a hopeless man in life, and should rather have led him to his death and opened up to him the pleasant West, that West where he would be under the guardianship of the gods.

The soul at first replies in some words in which she seems to refuse absolutely to accompany him; but the unhappy man immediately answers that he will on no account go alone to the tomb. He will take his soul with him, for his lot, and hers too, is to die, and his name alone ought to exist; the West ought to become his dwelling-place. She has nothing, besides, to fear; she will be as happy as he who is in his pyramid, and as he to whom a living man on earth has rendered funeral honours; she will not be like other souls that suffer weariness, heat, or hunger. "If thou wilt guide me so to death, thou wilt never regret being lodged in the West. So, my soul, my brother, be the one to pay me the last honours, to make the funeral sacrifices, to keep by the bark on the day of the funeral and to prepare the funeral bier.[1] Then my soul opens her mouth and replies to what I have said: 'If thou art thinking of thy funeral, it is only affliction, it is that which makes tears flow, and distresses human beings, and causes a man to rush out of his house and throw himself on the ground; thou wilt then no more rise again to behold the light of the sun. Those who build with granite

[1] The whole piece has been translated by Professor Erman.

and erect their beautiful pyramids with splendid work,—those who surround themselves with walls as do the gods,—their tables of offerings are as empty as those of the wretch that dies on the canal bank. . . . Hearken to me; it is good for a man to hearken; celebrate a happy day, and throw aside thy cares. . . .'

"Then I open my mouth and I reply thus to what my soul has said." The unhappy man now begins to speak in language which I suppose we ought to call poetry, if we may judge from its constantly repeated refrains: "Behold ye, my name is odious; behold ye, more than the odour of birds on a summer day when the sky is burning hot. Behold ye, my name is more odious than the odour of a fisherman coming from the marsh after fishing. Behold ye, my name is more odious than the odour of a crocodile. Behold ye, my name is more odious than the woman to her husband when she has been spoken falsely of. To whom shall I speak to-day? My brothers are perverted, and the friends of to-day are no longer faithful. To whom shall I speak to-day? Hearts are full of pride, and each one seizes his neighbour's goods. To whom shall I speak to-day? The mild man goes to his ruin, and the violent man has access to all men. To whom shall I speak to-day? The wretched man is faithful while the brother who is with him becomes his foe. To whom shall I speak to-day? People have no remembrance of yesterday; that which I have done is in a moment as if it had not been. To whom shall I speak to-day? I am full of misery, and the faithful man is no more. To whom shall I speak to-day? Evil smites the earth, and there is no end to it. Death is before me to-day, even as the return of health to the sick, when one escapes from sickness. Death is before me to-day, like the perfume of myrrh, like sitting down in the shelter of the sail on a windy day. Death is before me to-day, like the smell of the lotus, and like reclining on the bench in the land of intoxica-

DIALOGUE OF A MAN WITH HIS SOUL   201

tion. Death is before me to-day as he who yearns to see his home again after he has spent long years in captivity. He who is *over there* is mighty as a living god who punishes crime in the person of him who has committed it. He who is *over there* will be kept in the bark of Ra, and will offer choice victims in the temples. He who is *over there* is like a wise man whom no one hinders from directing his speech to Ra.

"Then my soul says to me: 'Cease thy complaints . . . . if I have refused thee so far, thou wilt yet reach the West. Thy members will go into the ground, I will remain there after thou shalt have found thy rest. Let us together make an abode.'" Thus the soul who appeared so inexorable at the outset consents to yield, and the hopeless man attains the much-desired rest.

We have here travelled a long way from the brilliant descriptions of the other-world delights of an older time. Yet in the foregoing we find, in the soul's first utterances, the echo of a tendency which may be traced through the whole course of Egyptian history. From the most remote epochs we can detect a totally different school of thought—one which we should style pessimistic or even materialistic, whose maxim is: "There is nothing but the present life; let us enjoy the present hour, for after death we have only misery to expect." This tendency runs parallel with the teaching of the Book of the Dead, and it shows itself at a remarkable point. On the funeral day the relatives and friends of the defunct are seated at a banquet more or less sumptuous, according to the rank of the deceased; and musicians and harpers are summoned to the feast to sing and play. We have several versions of the harper's song, differing in date by almost three thousand years; it is a text, therefore, which might be called canonical, and the root idea is always the same, *carpe diem*, "seize the passing hour," "enjoy life," for in the next world there is nothing to look forward

EGYPTIAN PESSIMISM

to but sadness and deception. Here is the oldest version that has come down to us, dating from the time of King Antef, nearly three thousand years before our era:[1] "Whilst one body decays, others live on, since the time of the ancestors. The gods who existed aforetime—they are like the mummies and the shades that are lying in their tombs. Dwellings were built for them, but now there is no more place for them. See! what have they become? I have listened to the words of Imhotep and of Hortetef, whom people sing and celebrate on every side: look at the place where they were; its walls are in ruins, their place no longer exists, they are as if they had never been, no one comes to celebrate what they were, to celebrate their opulence, to incline our heart to let them conduct us to the place whither they have gone. Pacify thy heart by making it forget, and be happy by following thy heart as long as thou livest. Put perfumes on thy head; array thyself in

[1] Translated by M. Maspero.

fine linen, make use of what is most precious in what is offered to the gods. Spare not to enjoy thyself. Do not cease to follow thy heart, and afflict not thy heart so long as thou art on earth, until the day arrive when lament will be made for thee and when he whose heart beats no more hears not the lamentations. Tears can in no way revive the heart of him who is in the tomb. So celebrate a joyful day, and do not depart from it. Lo, no one is permitted to carry away his goods with him; yea, no one returns again who is gone thither."

Here is another instance, of a much later time, since it dates from the Greek kings; but it is still more poignant, I would even say more tragic. It treats of a woman who was happy and keeps telling us so. She recounts on her large funerary stele that when she was fourteen years of age her father gave her in marriage to the high priest of Ptah. Thrice she became a mother, but she had no son, no one to succeed her husband in his high offices.

Then the pair addressed their petition to the god Imhotep, son of Ptah, who hears prayers and grants sons to those who have none. The god appeared to the priest in a dream, and ordered him to do certain pieces of work in the god's sanctuary, in return for which he (the god) would give him a son. On awakening, the high priest immediately assembled his subordinates and the most skilful workmen he could find. The work was accomplished, and on the fifth of the month Epiphi the priestess gave birth to a son, who was called Imhotep. "Four years afterwards came the day when I was carried to the tomb. My husband the high priest laid me in the cemetery, he granted me all the rites, he gave me a splendid funeral, and he laid me in his tomb, behind Alexandria." After this recital of the story of her life and her sumptuous burial, let us now hear her last exhortations, addressed to posterity: "O Father, Husband, Relative, Priest, cease not to drink, to eat, to drain the cup of pleasure and of love, and to hold joyous festival; follow thy heart day and night, and suffer not sorrow to pierce thy heart through all the years thou shalt spend on earth. For the West is a land of sleep and darkness, an oppressive abode for those who dwell in it. They sleep, they are motionless forms; they never wake again to look on their brethren; they know not their father or their mother; their heart yearns not for their spouses or their children. The living water which earth holds for any one who inhabits it, is for me but a stagnant pool. . . . I no longer know where I am since I came into this valley. Oh! if I had only running water to drink; oh! if my face were but turned towards the breeze of the north on the water's brink. Perchance it would refresh my heart and quiet my torment," and so forth. So there were in Egypt some desolate hearts who could not behold, without terror, the day approaching when they should have to leave this world. I love to think, however, that they were few in number, and that the vast majority of the people were more ready to repeat these other words, full of hope, addressed to Ra, the great god: " I come to thee, I follow with thee to behold thy disc every day. I am not shut in, I am not repulsed. My members are renewed at the splendour of thy beauties, like all thy faithful ones, for I am one of those who are thy favoured ones on earth. I am come to the land of the ages, I rejoin the land of eternity. Thou, O Ra, behold what thou hast wished for me that I may be even as a god!"

V

Do not expect from Egypt charming myths like those that we find in the Greek poetry. Myths there are, and we are acquainted with several which have been preserved to us in all their details; but a large number betray their existence only in scattered allusions in the Pyramid Texts or in the Book of the Dead. As, however, we find but a single feature or a phrase indicating their presence, it is impossible to reconstruct the whole from such slender material. Indeed, it would be surprising if there were no myths in Egypt, for they answer to one of the characteristics of the Egyptian mind. A man of the time of the Thothmes family or of the Ramessides was not a sad mortal, for ever preoccupied with the thought of his death and burial, as we are sometimes tempted to think. He was not afraid of gaiety and merriment; he loved music and dancing; and in literature he appreciated the tale with a historical kernel, or, more frequently, with a dash of the marvellous in it. Thus we can understand how his imagination would lend itself to fashion the life of the gods and invent episodes to garnish it, or adventures which might befall them. And so, as I said at the beginning, though these legends possess none of the charm of those in Homer or in Hesiod, they are yet very interesting, because they bring the anthropomorphic character of the gods into bolder relief than do the hymns or the magical formulæ. The legends are of two kinds —one dealing with the relations of gods with men; the other, with the sayings and doings of the gods among themselves. Let us begin with the first category, from which we shall gain some knowledge of the feelings which the gods at times evinced towards human beings.

One of the longest and most complete of these myths is that of the Destruction of Mankind by the gods. It is found in two of the royal tombs of the nineteenth and twentieth dynasties. We are transported to Heliopolis, the religious capital of Egypt. There, the first King Ra has reigned for many long years, yet he has not grown grey, for his hair is of true lapis lazuli. Now, as blue was in Egypt the conventional colour for black, this means that the hair of his head was still the colour of ebony; his bones were of silver, and his flesh of gold. He suddenly learns that men have uttered blasphemous words against him. Then he addresses his court and says: "Summon to my presence Shu, Tafnout, Keb, Nout, and the fathers and the mothers who were with me when I was still in Nou, and I charge Nou to bring his companions with him. Bring them softly that men may not notice it, and their heart be not terrified. You will go with them into the great temple when they shall have given

THE DESTRUCTION OF MANKIND 211

their consent. . . ." When the gods had arrived at the place, they bowed down in presence of his majesty, and they said in his presence: "Speak unto us thy words that we may hear them."

We see here that the gods live and move about on the earth like human beings, who, at times, can see them and manifest their fear. The assembly of the gods, or rather the family council, is held in the great temple of Heliopolis. What is going to be the result of their deliberations?

Said by Ra to Nou: "O Thou, the eldest of the gods, of whom I am born; and ye ancestral gods, lo! mankind, who were born from mine eye, utter words against me. Tell me what ye would do in this matter? Behold I have waited, and I have not slain them, before I had heard what ye had to say." Said by the majesty of Nou: "O my son Ra, thou who art greater than he that made him, and than those who formed him, thy throne is stablished sure, and great is the fear thou dost inspire; let thine eye alone, be turned upon those who conspire against Thee." Said by the majesty of Ra: " Behold they flee to the mountains, and their hearts are dismayed by reason of what they have said." Then spake they (the gods) with one voice in the presence of the majesty of Ra: "Only let thine eye go forth; it will overcome those who hatch base designs against thee . . . . let it descend in the form of Hathor." In this fashion the eye of the god becomes the goddess Hathor. When the goddess returns after slaying mankind on the mountains, the majesty of this god says: "Come in peace, Hathor!" . . . . The goddess replies: "Thou art alive; when I triumphed over mankind, my heart has rejoiced over it." But she proceeds with her work of destruction, for it is stated that for several nights she wades in the blood of mankind, starting from Heracleopolis. Ra begins to be afraid that the massacre is only too complete, and bestirs himself to save the residue of mankind, and here is the means to which he

THE DESTRUCTION OF MANKIND 213

has recourse: "Said by Ra: 'I summon to me messengers light and swift; let them speed like wind . . .'" The messengers arrived at once. His majesty said to them: "Let them run to Elephantiné, and let them bring me mandrakes in great number." When the mandrakes were brought, they were sent on to the grinder, or miller who dwells in Heliopolis, to grind them, while the priestesses crushed barley to make a drink, the fruits were put into the vessels with the human blood, and there were filled with this drink seven thousand jars.

"Then came the majesty of Ra with his gods to see this drink, after he had spoken to the goddess about slaying mankind. Said by the majesty of Ra: 'It is well; I am going to protect mankind with this. Give your voice on this. I will no more bid her to slay mankind." But the goddess had already departed, and it appears it was not possible to stop her—at least she must be made harmless, and this is the device resorted to: "The majesty of Ra gave orders to pour out the water which was in these jars, under cover of night, and the fields were covered with the water to the depths of four palms, according to the will of the god. The goddess comes in the morning and finds the fields flooded with water; she admires her beautiful face in it, and begins to drink to satiety; she went about intoxicated, and she recognised mankind no more. Said by the majesty of Ra: 'Come in peace, charming goddess.'" And in memory of this event were instituted various ceremonies in the cult of Hathor. Such is the stratagem. Ra does not dare to stop Hathor himself; he provides her with the means of getting intoxicated, and then she does not see mankind, and so they escape.

Behold, then, Ra satisfied, as one would suppose, with his work; he had decided to take vengeance on mankind, and he succeeded so well that he had to interpose to prevent their total destruction. Nothing then seems to be wanting to his satisfaction; quite the contrary, he is more discontented than ever. Said by the majesty of Ra: "I have a sharp pain which torments me; what, then, is wrong with me? Truly I am alive, but my heart is weary of being together with men. I have not destroyed them; it is not destruction that my might has dealt them." Said by the gods who are of his following: "Away with thy weariness; thou hast obtained all that thou didst desire." But Ra insists: "My members have been in pain a long time, and I am unable to walk until I get another to help me."

Then Nou commands Shu and Tafnout to come to his help; and on the recommendation of her father, Nout the goddess resolves to carry Ra on her back. For this purpose she takes the form of a cow. At this juncture night comes on, but in the morning men sally forth, bow in hand; and it is probable that they make an offer to Ra to fight his enemies. The god also delivers himself of these interesting words: "Your sins are behind you (forgiven); slaughter averteth slaughter, hence arise sacrifices." If this interpretation of a phrase in which several signs are wanting be correct, the conception which led to the institution of sacrifice among the Egyptians is the same as among the Hebrews or the Greeks: slaughter averteth slaughter, death removes or puts away death. Men had rebelled against their lord; they are then doomed to destruction; but some of them obtain pardon by putting to death those that persist in rebellion; and henceforth sacrifices arise to commemorate the event which saved mankind from total destruction. Under this uncouth apparel, therefore, lies an idea which deserves to be taken into consideration.

Ra reaches the sky borne on the cow, and in order to testify to his gratitude to her he gives free scope to his creative power. He first calls into existence the Field of Aalou, and makes plants grow in it; then he places in it as its inhabitants beings of every kind, which hang from the sky, even the stars.

CREATION OF SKY AND STARS 217

"Then Nout begins to tremble, because of the height." Ra, addressing Shu, says to him: "Take with thee my daughter Nout, and watch over the multitudes who live in the nightly sky; place them upon thy head and be their foster-father." Shu and Nout thus become the guardians of all the beings of the sky; and this is the reason why the cow of Nout is called the "multitude of beings": and Shu becomes a sort of Atlas, holding up with his two hands and head the body of the cow carrying all the stars.

By this strange myth, then, we return to the cosmogony of Heliopolis: Ra springs from Nout, but he is the father of Shu and Nout; the latter is the sky, and she is supported by the powerful arms of Shu, who helps her in bearing the burden of all the stars.

Next, Ra addresses Keb, bidding him to watch with care over the reptiles of land and water; finally, he speaks to a god who is his favourite, and who does not figure in the Ennead of Heliopolis, namely, Thoth. He tells Thoth that he will become "his abode," or, as Erman translates it, "his deputy": it will be his duty to give light to the lower sky, standing therefore for the moon. Ra then allots various symbols to the god Thoth, *e.g.* the ibis, the dog-ape, the lunar disc, and the crane.

Here, then, we have a story which begins with an account of the rebellion of mankind against Ra, and ends with the creation of the heavens and the moon. It is a good example of the incoherence that reigns in Egyptian conceptions. The book, besides, is a very holy book, and ought not to be read by anyone without preparatory ceremonies. "He who utters these words," it is said, "ought to anoint himself with balm and fine oil, and have a censer in his hands"; and after other minute prescriptions the rubric adds: "When Thoth wishes to read this book for Ra, he purifies himself by nine days' purifications, and priests and men ought to do the same." It is probably for this reason that the book is found hidden away in little niches at the back of the tomb, in places certainly not easily got at by the first comer.

Now, to this feature alone we might point as constituting a fundamental difference between the Egyptian myth and the Greek myth. The Egyptian myth is not a story meant for all the world to read, or intended to be a subject for the play of a poet's fancy: it is, on the one hand, a sacred book, and therefore the object of special veneration, and, on the other hand, it is a magical text endowed with peculiar virtues, to which we shall afterwards allude. A comparison has been made between the Egyptian story of the Destruction of Mankind and other legends, or even with the story of the Deluge in the Book of Genesis. In the latter case it is not possible to establish any real resemblance. In the Egyptian myth the earth is covered with water, not for the purpose of destroying the human race, but, on the contrary, of saving it. The one feature common to both stories is the desire of the Creator God to destroy his own work, which, in the Egyptian narrative, is, as Ra says, the work of his eye.

But in another story, taken from the Book of the Dead, we find a closer analogy with the Biblical story of the Deluge. It occurs in a very rare chapter, of which we have only two very incomplete versions. Probably we have in it a myth originating in Heracleopolis, in Middle Egypt. It consists of a dialogue between the deceased and various divinities, especially Toum. To one of the deceased's questions Toum replies in these words: "Lo! I am about to deface that which I have made. The earth will become water through an inundation, as it was at the beginning. I shall be the only one left remaining along with Osiris, and I will take the form of a little serpent which no man knows and no god can see. I am going to benefit Osiris; I will give him power over the lower world, and his son Horus will inherit his throne in the island of flames."

Here we have a real deluge, that is, a destruction of everything upon the earth by the action of water, and this water is not an uninterrupted rain lasting many days; it will all at once rise up of itself like a mighty inundation, and convert the earth into an ocean. The sole surviving being will be Toum, who will not be king himself. He will hide, and conceal himself from observation like a little serpent; it is Osiris who will become king, and his throne will be so surely established that he will hand on the sovereignty to Horus, his son. Osiris will be able to do what he wills on earth, so that Horus will come to sit in his place, and he himself will take possession of his place of rest. The cosmogony here is somewhat different from that of Heliopolis. Toum disappears; Osiris takes the first place; the human Osiris dies, and to him succeeds his son, Horus. All this clearly shows that we have to do with a myth of Heracleopolis, whose great god was Osiris surnamed "the terrible." This is the reason why the Greeks translated his name by Heracles (Hershefi, the terrible, Arsaphes). The rest of the piece consists of broken lines without beginning or end; they point to a contest with Set; mention is made of "the blood which flows at Heracleopolis," and Ra speaks to Osiris: "Great is the fear which thou dost inspire. I have increased the terror which thou causest." One fact stands out from this myth, and it is this: that Toum himself, at the beginning, destroyed what he had created, in order to make way for Osiris.

Here, again, is another myth, which explains why swine are not sacrificed to Horus, and why two of his sons are allotted to the North of Egypt and two to the South. The myth in this case has no connection with cosmogony, but with worship. A disaster happens to Horus in consequence of some presumption on his part towards his father, in wishing to be his equal. The myth comes from the Book of the Dead. The deceased speaks as follows: "Do you know for what purpose the North

SACRIFICE OF SWINE FORBIDDEN

has been given to Horus? I know it, if ye do not know it. It was Ra who gave it to him in amends for the wound which Horus received in the eye, in this wise: Horus spoke thus to Ra, 'Suffer me to see the beings which thine eye has created, as Ra himself sees them.' Then Ra replies to Horus: 'Look then yonder at that black pig.' He looked, and behold a grievous mishap afflicted his eye. Then Horus says to Ra: 'My eye is as though a blow had been given me by Set,' and (translating literally) 'he ate his heart'—that is, he regretted bitterly his foolish or imprudent request made to Ra. Then Ra says to the gods: 'Lay Horus upon his bed; perchance he will recover.' It was, of course, Set who had taken the form of a black pig, and he caused a smarting wound in the eye of Horus. Then Ra spoke thus to the gods: 'The pig will be an abomination to Horus if he gets well.' Hence it comes that the pig is an abomination to Horus. And all the gods round about him said: 'From the time that Horus was a child they made sacrifices of gazelles and pigs to him; the pig will now be an abomination to the gods who are round about him. As to the four gods whose father is Horus and whose mother is Isis, Horus spoke thus to Ra: Give me two of them for the North and two for the South; they are of my body; let them be with me for an eternal duration.'"

This, then, is the reason why swine are no longer sacrificed to Horus—because he once imprudently asked of his father to see, as his father saw, the beings whom his father had created. Ra, very wisely, lets him have a trial, inviting him to look at a black pig; but the unlucky Horus feels a violent pain in his eye. The pig was simply Set in disguise, and poor Horus could do nothing but repent bitterly of having wished to exalt himself to the height of Ra. The Egyptian conclusion of the myth is that since that day swine were no longer sacrificed to Horus. We might almost extract a moral from it, as from a fable, on the dangers of presumption.

MYTH OF RA AND ISIS

We have just discussed two cosmogony myths which deal with great events—the one accounting for the creation of the sky and the stars, or the transformation of the face of the earth; the other giving us the reason why certain victims were proscribed in sacrifice. Let us now take a myth of another kind, one which treats of magical or rather medical performances. It is intended to enhance the effect of a remedy. Something happens to Ra; and, as we shall see, the myth shows that the gods have no great respect for one another. Isis has no scruple in playing a trick on the Lord of the World, in order to better her position, which seems to have been very much like that of any woman living on earth.

" Now[1] Isis was a woman clever of speech, and her heart being weary of the multitude of mankind, she preferred the multitude of the gods, and she highly esteemed the multitude of the spirits: might she not be the equal of Ra in the heavens and the earth, and be

[1] Translated by Lefébure.

mistress of the world—so she meditated in her heart—if she only knew the name of the venerable god?" This name was a secret, a mystery—and we shall see why she was so keen to know it. "Now Ra came every day at the head of his boatmen, and installed himself on the throne of the two horizons. But the god had grown old, and his saliva ran down to the ground. And Isis kneaded it with her hand, together with the earth on it, and of this she made a sacred serpent, to which she gave the shape of a dart. It did not stand erect and living before her face; she left it lying upon the road on which the great god was wont to pass, according to the desire of his heart, in his double realm.

"The venerable god went forth, the gods of this Pharaoh in his train. Then he walked as he did every day, and the sacred serpent bit him. . . . The god opens his mouth, and the cry of his majesty reached unto the heavens. His divine cycle said: 'What is that?' and his gods cried out, 'What is there?' But

Ra could not answer; his jaw-bones rattled; all his members shivered; the venom took possession of his flesh, as the Nile takes possession of his domain. When the great god had strengthened his heart, he cried to those in his following: 'Come to me, children of my members, gods that came forth from me, that I may cause you to know what has happened. I have been pierced through by something malignant—my heart knoweth that; but my eyes have not seen it, my hand has not done it, and I know not what I ought to do. I have never felt pain like it; there is nothing more malignant than this. I am a prince, the son of a prince, the being sprung from a god; I am great, the son of a great one; my father thought out my name; I am he who has a host of names, and a multitude of forms; my being exists in every god. Toum and Horus have addressed their praises to me; my father and my mother uttered my name, but it was concealed in my breast by him who begat me, so that no magician may gain the mastery over me by his enchantments.

"'Lo! I had gone forth from my dwelling to behold what I had made, and was walking in the world which I had created, when something stung me, I know not what—it is not fire, it is not water, and yet my heart is a pan of fire, my flesh quivers, and my members are seized with shaking. I beseech you bring me those of my children and of the gods whose words are kind, whose mouth is wise and whose skill reacheth the sky.' When his children came, each of the gods present wept over him; but Isis came with her sorceries, with her mouth full of the breath of life, with her incantations to heal afflictions, and her words to make dead throats live. She says: 'What is it, then, divine father; what is this? A serpent has sent suffering into thee; a creature of thine has lifted up his head against thee? Truly he shall be overwhelmed by my beneficent charms. I will make him yield at the sight of thy rays.' The aged one

THE DEVICE OF ISIS

begins to tell over again what had befallen him; he describes afresh all the ills that torment him. 'Water,' he says, 'streams down my face as in the summer time.' Then Isis says to Ra: 'Tell me then thy name, divine father, for that person lives who is called by his name.' We see that the crafty goddess does not forget what she is aiming at getting. But Ra does not yield all at once; he tries to reply evasively, and he begins a speech which is not wanting in a kind of poetry: 'I am he who made the heavens and the earth, who reared aloft the mountains and created everything that is upon it. I am he who made the water and created the great deep. I am he who created the heavens and hidden in them the two horizons, and placed therein the souls of the gods. I am he who when he opens his eyes produces the light, and when he closes them produces darkness; who makes the waters of the Nile to rise, when he giveth the command. But the gods do not know his name. I am he who makes the hours and gives birth to the days; it is I who open the festivals of the year and create the inundation. I am he who causes the flame of life to rise so as to permit the labours of the field. I am Khepera in the morning, Ra at his noon, and Toum in the evening.' The god ceases, but his words are without effect; the poison is not arrested in its progress, and the god is not relieved. Isis has no pity for him; she remains implacable. 'Thy name,' she says, 'has not been mentioned in what thou hast just said; tell it to me, and I will expel the poison, for he who is called by his name lives.' Yet the poison burned like fire, it was fiercer than the flame of a furnace. Thus spake the majesty of Ra: 'I consent to be searched out by Isis; my name shall come forth from my body into her body.' Then the god became invisible before the gods, his place was empty in the bark of millions of years. When the time came that his heart, which concealed the mysterious name, went forth, the goddess said to her son Horus: 'Bind the god by an oath that he will also give me his two eyes.'

"When his name was taken away from the great god, Isis, the great magician, said: 'Run out, poisons, come forth from Ra; O Eye of Horus, come forth from the god and sparkle outside his mouth. It is I who have worked, it is I who caused the mighty poison to descend to the ground. Verily the name of the great god hath been taken from him. Ra is alive, and the poison is dead.'"

Here ends the story, and we do not know whether Isis is content with the place she has conquered for herself among the gods—she who alone succeeded in healing Ra. Nothing more is told us, for we are now introduced to some words of magic, the origin of which is given in the tale: "So-and-so, son of Mistress So-and-so, will live, the poison will die: that is what the great Isis, queen of the gods, says; she who knew Ra by his own name." These are the important words whose virtue will be beneficent, to be said over images of Toum,

Isis, and Horus. The fact of having pronounced these words in their presence or, as the Egyptian has it, "over them," will impart to these images the power of dispelling the poison of serpents; they are amulets or talismans whose curative virtues or properties will be infallible. But it is not only the images whose power the words will increase; the remedies used will show their good effects. For this is the prescription at the close: "Put it, having written it down, into a liquid to be swallowed by a person. Inscribe it in the same way on a piece of linen, and lay it on his neck. It is an effectual remedy. Make a drink of beer or of wine to be drunk by the person afflicted. It is the destruction of the poison, perfectly and for ever."

I said above that this tale has a medical purpose, as we are informed, indeed, in so many words. The first myth was religious in its nature, and meant to be used for the benefit of a deceased person, so that, when it was read and all the prescribed ceremonies were performed, the favour of the gods was probably secured for him. The same myth also gives us information on the origin of several ceremonies. The other myth we have considered contains no religious element; it is simply a magician's myth—we might almost say, a charlatan's. It is for the use of " So-and-so, son of So-and-so "—any person whatever.

And yet it still preserves the chief features of the same sort of pantheistic teaching which we have noticed elsewhere. The gods are quite anthropomorphic: Isis is a woman, Ra an old man, with all the infirmities of age; nevertheless, he is still the creator of all things; his being exists in every god; and his power manifests itself in all his works, which embrace the whole world and all that it contains.

The myth of Isis healing Ra is very analogous to others found on amulets and designed for the protection of their owner from different evils, especially from the bite of serpents or of scorpions. These are the specially magical myths. In general the subject is Isis and the death of her son Horus, who was the victim of one of these perfidious reptiles. This is the tale as it was told in the time of King Nectanebo :[1]

"I am Isis; I conceived and brought forth Horus; I the goddess, I brought Horus into the world, the son of Osiris, in the marshes of Athou. I rejoiced greatly, for I saw that he would take his father's place. I hid him carefully for fear that he should be stung. I went to the city of Am; I was hailed as of old, and I delayed to look for the child and to bring him his food. I returned to embrace Horus; and I found my Horus, my precious gold, my new-born, as if he were no more; he had wet the ground with the tears of his eyes and the froth of his lips; his body was stiff; his heart was still; no muscle of his limbs moved. I uttered a cry of despair: 'It is I, it is I . . . '"—what she said is so much destroyed that it cannot be translated. . . .

[1] Translated by Golénischeff and Brugsch.

"I then summoned some people, and verily they turned their hearts to me; I summoned also the inhabitants of the marshes, and they came about me immediately: the people came to me from their houses, and they drew near, hearing my voice. They too uttered laments over my great misfortune, but none of them opened the mouth to speak, for every one of them showed a great grief, but none of them knew how to restore the life.

"And there came from the city a woman, well known and of rank in her district: she came to me to restore the life, her heart was quite full of that, but my son Horus remained motionless." It is difficult to understand the words that come next; it would seem as if there was a conversation between the two women, and they succeed in discovering that a scorpion had stung the child. The poor mother's despair knew no bounds; she puts her nose in the mouth of her son to find out if he still breathes; she opens the wound, and discovers that it contains poison; then she takes the child in her arms, and begins to skip about—we should say, like a madwoman—but the Egyptians say, like a fish thrown on the fire, shrieking, "O Ra, he is stung, thy son Horus; he is stung, thy son; he is stung, the heir of heirs, the master of the royal diadem, the innocent, the child of the gods, for whom I was getting what was needful." The poor mother is moving, even eloquent, in her sorrow: "Then came Nephthys and wept, and her lamentations resounded through all the land; and Selk too, who asked again and again, 'What then has happened to thy son Horus? O Isis, direct thy prayer to the heavens, and then the boatmen of Ra will stop, and the bark of Ra will go forward no more; for the sake of thy son Horus it will come to a halt.'" Isis lifts up her voice to the heavens, and she entreats the eternal bark. The sun came to a standstill when the request reached him, and the bark did not stir from its place, but Thoth arrived equipped with his enchantments, carrying his formula of

MIRACLE OF HEALING BY THOTH

victory, and says: "O Isis, glorious goddess, whose mouth is wise, thy son Horus has come to no ill, for his protection belongs to the bark of Ra. I am come to-day from the bark of the solar disc, from the place where it was yesterday when night came and when light disappeared, to the end that I might heal Horus for his mother, and every other like sufferer."

Then Isis the goddess spake thus: "O Thoth, great is thy heart; but hast thou not delayed in thy purpose; comest thou equipped with all thine enchantments, and carriest thou the formula which will triumph over anything, for one knows not the number of . . . ?" "Fear not, O goddess Isis; lament not, Nephthys. I am come from the sky to restore the child alive to his mother. *Horus! Horus! be thy heart strengthened, and succumb not to the fire of the poison.* Horus is saved, like him who is in his disc, and who enlightens the land with the splendour of his eyes; saved, too, is every sufferer. Saved is Horus the first-born of the sky, he who gives their forms to those that are and that shall be"; and the god goes on to give utterance to appropriate formulæ whose effect will be the revival of the child. The last lines of the text are obscure, but they contain, however, these words which Thoth addresses to Isis: "I am Thoth, the eldest of the sons of Ra. Toum and the cycle of the gods have charged me to give Horus back safe and sound to his mother, and to heal likewise every suffering being. Horus! Horus! thy double is thy protector, and thy form is thy safeguard; the venom is dead, and its fire is destroyed."

Then Isis, in gratitude, requests Thoth to extend his benefits to the inhabitants of the region of Buto, as they had begged with strong supplications that the son should be restored to his mother; and also that they should share in the life and healing which the power of Thoth could bring. Thoth grants her petition. "I bring joy," he says, "to those who are in the Sekti bark, the solar bark which was stopped.

Horus has been given back alive to his mother, Isis, and likewise every sick person will be given back alive to his mother, for the poison is dead, and its strength is gone."

These last lines reveal to us the aim and purpose of the myth: it is a talisman for the people of Buto against the stings of scorpions and serpents. If anyone has it in his house, engraved on a stele or other monument, it will be the best preservative against the bites of these formidable creatures. We thus see that the Egyptian myth is not an independent story which one enjoys in and for itself, for its literary or artistic value. It is always motived by something; it goes along with a ceremony of which it is the explanation, and it has a magical value. This is why it is to be read, or why people must have the text of it in their houses or about them.

But anthropomorphism, though seen chiefly in the myths, is found elsewhere also. The direct action of the divine powers on human beings, and their intervention in the life of man, are not seen exclusively in magic: the gods have other means of making their will known. They hold converse with men in many ways; they are fond, for instance, of revealing themselves in dreams. The belief in dreams as a channel of divine communication is present indeed in almost all religions, and in Egypt there were interpreters of dreams who, as well as the magicians, belonged to the college of the priests. There are stories extant of several dreams in which kings heard the voices of the gods and received divine directions. For instance, King Thothmes IV. is hunting in the desert, opposite Heliopolis, in the district which we now call Ghizeh; and being overcome by the heat of the sun and fatigue, he falls asleep at midday in the shadow of a gigantic monument, which is still the wonder of travellers, the great Sphinx. The story runs:[1] " And his majesty found that the god was speaking to him with his own mouth, as a father speaks to his son." The

[1] Translated by Maspero.

THE COMPLAINT OF THE SPHINX 241

god is the Sphinx himself, the emblem of the god Harmachis; it is, then, the statue which speaks to the king: "'See thou me, my son Thothmes, for I am thy father Harmachis, and I will grant thee to be king on my throne, a prince among the living, wearing the red crown and the white crown, as the chief of the gods possessing the land in all its length and breadth, the splendour of the eye of the lord of all things. I will place at thy disposal revenues from all the land of Egypt, abundant tribute, and a period of years, during which thou shalt be the chosen one of Ra; for my face will be turned towards thee, and thy face will be turned towards me, and thy heart will be inclined towards me. Now look at my fate! so that thou mayest be able to protect my beautiful members. The sand of the desert on which I am has surrounded me; I have decreed that thou shalt execute what is in my heart, for thou art my son, my protector. Come near; I am with thee; I am thy father.' When the prince heard these words he was greatly astonished, and he perceived that they were the words of this god." Unfortunately, the stele containing this text is broken here, and the narrative ends.

This tale, for it is one, is interesting in many respects. It shows us what kind of relations existed between gods and men. The god is nowhere shown in the imposing majesty we should expect to find in the case of the Sun: no, he is quite humble; he appeals to his son like a suppliant. The poor Sphinx was then, as now, unceasingly threatened with the enveloping sand of the desert, covering his enormous body, and only allowing his head and back to be seen. He would like well to be disencumbered of his covering, and to display himself in all his splendour; and for this he must supplicate the king to construct some defensive work to keep off the sand. This is his dearest wish, but he hardly ventures to make it known. He tries indeed to appeal to the filial affection due to him from Thothmes; yet he must needs begin by making magnificent promises: he himself will place him upon the throne; he will grant him a long and glorious reign; all the riches of Egypt and of foreign lands will flow into his treasury. In return for this brilliant future which he pledges himself to secure to Thothmes, the latter must undertake to clear the sand away entirely from the image of the god, and prevent its invasion from hiding from human view a large portion of the divine one's person. The two sides of the bargain, it will be seen, are not equal, for Thothmes has certainly the lion's share. The characteristic thing is the mercantile spirit which governs the relations of gods and men. A god does not believe, apparently, in his right to ask anything from man, unless he gives, I will not say the equivalent, but far more than he gets in return. Man, however, on his part, will not hesitate to put forward claims based simply on the feeling of gratitude which the god ought to have towards him.

We have a curious example of the same thing on another occasion, when Amon goes to the assistance of the king. It is a piece of writing which its first translator, E. de Rougé, called a poem; and certainly, though we are unacquainted with the rhythm of Egyptian verse, the style of the piece, its imaginative power, and the richness and exuberance of certain of its descriptions fully warrant the name.

Its subject is Rameses II., a prince who has long enjoyed a fictitious prestige. For long he has been regarded as the greatest of the kings of Egypt, surpassing in power all the other sovereigns. But the better we learn to know him, his halo of glory fades the more, and we can safely affirm that Rameses was a pompous, ostentatious monarch, whose sole aim seems to have been to dazzle posterity as well as his contemporaries; and also, that his too prolonged reign was really the beginning of Egyptian decadence. We must thank him, however, for having left us the work of the poet Pentaour, to which he attached great importance, since not only had he the work

A BARGAINING PRAYER

copied on papyrus, but also caused it to be engraved several times on temple walls. It tells how he was at war with the Kheta, a people of Syria. Whether from incapacity on his part, or through a stratagem of the enemy, he finds himself suddenly surrounded by countless hosts of the Kheta, including two thousand five hundred chariots cutting off his retreat. He is quite alone in his chariot, except for his charioteer. The king then calls on Amon, and the god is not deaf to his appeal. He comes to his aid in person; he speaks to the king; he shows himself to Rameses and imparts to him the aspect of a god, thus striking terror into the hearts of his enemies, who are put to rout. How does the voice of the god make itself heard? What is the god like? We do not know; let us remember that it is poetry we are reading. But the curious thing is the invocation Rameses makes. It is not a cry of distress, or an appeal to the helpful kindness of the god: he rather makes much of his rights, and counts up at great length, at such a critical moment, the claims he believes he has on the gratitude and recognition of the god, and only quite near the end of his petition does he allude to the love which Amon might have for him. It is the same spirit that animated Thothmes IV. when Harmachis made appeal to him. "Then his majesty says:[1] 'Who art thou, O my father Amon? does a father forget his son? Have I then done aught without thee? Have I not stept or staid, at thy word? I have not transgressed thy commands. Have I not consecrated numberless offerings to thee? I have filled thy holy abode with thy prisoners: I have built thee a temple for millions of years: I have given thee all my goods for thy storehouses: I have offered thee the whole world to enrich thy domains. I have sacrificed before thee thirty thousand cattle, with all wood of sweet scent. . . . I have built for thee pylons of stone, on to their completion, and I myself have set up their masts. I brought

[1] Translated by E. de Rougé.

thee obelisks from Elephantiné; 'tis I who had eternal stones carried (for thee)! Galleys are sailing on the sea for thee; they convey to thee the tributes of the nations. O verily! a wretched fate (is reserved) for him who opposes thy purposes; happiness awaits him who knows thee! for thy deeds come from a heart full of love. I call on thee, O my father Amon! Behold me in the midst of multitudes unknown to me; all nations are banded together against me, and I am alone by myself, no other is with me. My many soldiers have deserted me, none of my chariotry look at me, and when I call to them not one of them listens to my voice. But I find that Amon is worth more to me than a million of soldiers, than a hundred thousand of chariots, more than a myriad of brothers and children, were they all gathered in one. No works of many men avail: Amon will exceed them. I have done these things by the counsel of thy mouth, O Amon, and I have never transgressed thy counsels. Lo! have I not glorified thee to the furthest ends of the earth?—The voice rang as far as Hermonthis: Amon came at my call: he gives me his hand. I raise a shout of joy; he called to me behind: 'I am running to thy help, Rameses! I am with thee; it is I, thy father; my hand is with thee, and I am worth more to thee than hundreds of thousands. I am sovran lord of night, loving valour; I have found a heart that is courageous, and I am well pleased. My will shall be accomplished.—Like Month, on the right, I let fly my arrows; on the left I overwhelm them. I am like Baal in his hour, before them. The two thousand five hundred chariots that surround me are broken in pieces before my mares.'" Rameses then describes the slaughter which he made of his enemies, in whose eyes he appears to be a god. They say the one to the other: "It is not a mortal man who is in amongst us, it is Sutekh, the mighty warrior, it is Baal in bodily form. These are not the doings of a man, the things that he does; alone, all alone he hurls back

SPEAKING AND HEALING IMAGES 249

hundreds of thousands, without his chiefs, without his soldiers."

Here, then, we have instances of direct intervention by a god in the doings of a king. It must be noted that these narratives are not taken from religious books properly so called: the first is found in a tale, and the other in a poem.

We have seen, in our discussion of the myths, that they were read before statuettes or little figures which thereby acquired a supernatural power; these figures then became mediums of healing to which recourse was had for the cure of wounds or sickness. But the Egyptians went still further than this. Not only did they allow that the gods conversed with them,—not only did they read the incantations which Thoth was supposed to utter, as if the god himself were speaking,— but they also made statues speak; they possessed oracular or prophetic statues which intervened on many occasions in their lives.

This kind of statue was chiefly found at

Thebes, and in one of the holy places of the city, the temple of Khons. This sanctuary dates for the most part from the time of the last Ramesside kings, the twenty-first dynasty, the dynasty of the priest-kings, the high priests of Amon who succeeded so well in establishing themselves by the side of the king that they ended by dislodging him from the throne and occupying it themselves. Khons was originally the son of Amon and Mut; his worship was closely bound up with that of Amon; and we may well suppose that the priests of Amon readily employed the art—let us call it the fraud— of making statues speak, for the purpose of enhancing the prestige of their god, and consequently of themselves. At the close of the twentieth dynasty they invented a tale which was ascribed to the reign of Rameses II., and which relates how a request was made to one of the gods to go and exorcise a princess in Mesopotamia. What at once stamps the story as an invention is the fact

[*To face page* 250.

Khons-Neferhotep.   Mut and Amon   worshipped by the King.
(From Temple of Khons, Karnak.)

THE POSSESSED PRINCESS 251

that, at the beginning, it places Rameses II. in the country of the Naharin, in Mesopotamia, where we are told the princes of the whole earth came to bow themselves in his presence and to implore his favour. Now, according to what we know of his reign and campaigns, Rameses never went so far as Mesopotamia; he never got beyond Palestine and Syria.

However that may be, we are told that, while he was thus engaged, the prince of Bakhtan brought his daughter, a woman of very great beauty, to him, and the Pharaoh took her to Egypt as his wife and gave her the name of Ra-neferou (the beauties of Ra). Now, one day at Thebes, when he was holding a great festival in honour of Amon, he was informed of the arrival of an envoy from the prince of Bakhtan, bearing rich presents, who came to tell him that Queen Ra-neferou's sister, the young Bentresht, was very ill, and to say that the prince begged Rameses to send a man of skill to cure her. Rameses assembled all the wise men, the sacred scribes, the magicians, and desired them to choose from their number a skilful man to go to Bakhtan. The choice fell on a man named Thothemheb, who set out for Bakhtan, and found the princess possessed by a spirit. He is obliged to confess his inability. Yet we must believe that sufficient time was given him for trying all likely remedies, for it is only nine years after the dispatch of the first messenger that a second arrives urgently requesting the King to send a god this time. Then the King goes into the temple of Khons Neferhotep, one of the triad of Thebes, son of Amon and Mut. M. de Rougé translates the name Neferhotep by "quiet in his perfection": it might also be rendered "good and peaceable." The epithet indicates that the characteristic of the god is tranquillity, repose: he does not leave his abode, like others—he is not a warlike god. He issues his decrees without forsaking his Olympian calm. We shall keep to his name of Neferhotep in what follows.

Rameses asks from him authority to allow

THE POSSESSED PRINCESS

another god Khons, "He who makes or executes plans and drives out rebels," to go to Bakhtan, and requests the god to signify his consent by nodding his head, which the god immediately does, two several times. Rameses also asks the god "to send his protection with him" on the journey—a "protection" which, I believe, would be put forth by the double of the god, who, though invisible, would always be behind him, and the traveller would also receive the power required for healing the princess. Khons, "who-executes-plans," appears to me to be an emanation of the other Khons, perhaps a portion of his body, which has taken the form of the god. In the myth of the Destruction of Mankind we saw that the god Ra sent forth his eye, which assumed the appearance of Hathor. Khons-who-executes-plans is something analogous, with reference to Khons Neferhotep: he is the agent, he makes journeys, and the other god despatches him when his power must be put forth at a distance. We may suppose that Khons-who-executes-plans was a statue on which a magical virtue had been bestowed by certain words said over it or before it, like those which protected from or healed the bites of serpents. The special power of the statue was probably that of an exorcist, as appears from the other epithet, " he who expels the rebels," that is, he who expels everything opposed to the will of the gods.

The god sets out in his bark, which is carried on men's shoulders: in the bark is the shrine which contains his statue or his emblem. He is escorted by five smaller boats, a chariot and numerous horses of the West and East. We are not favoured with any details as to the events of the journey, which was happy if not rapid—for it lasted a year and five months. As the god approached his destination the prince of Bakhtan, with his nobles and soldiers, came to meet him; he threw himself on the ground before him, and bade him welcome. Khons repaired at once to the house of the princess, imparted to her his healing virtue, probably by laying his hand four times on her neck, and the princess was instantly relieved.

But the spirit or the demon that possessed her did not depart without a word.[1] The spirit which dwelt in her said, in the presence of Khons - who - executes - plans - in - Thebes: "Welcome, thou great god who drivest out the rebels; the city of Bakhtan is thine, its people are thy slaves, I am thy slave. I will go to the place whence I came, to satisfy thy heart concerning the matter of thy journey. Let thy majesty be pleased to command that a festival be celebrated in my honour by the prince of Bakhtan." The god nods to his priest, saying: "It behoves that the prince of Bakhtan make a rich offering to this spirit." While these things were happening, and while Khons - who - executes - plans - in - Thebes was talking with the spirit, the prince of Bakhtan stood with his army, seized with a very great fear. He caused a rich offering to be made to Khons as well as to the spirit, and he celebrated

[1] Translated by E. de Rougé.

a festival in their honour, whereupon the spirit departed peaceably whithersoever he wished. Great joy was in all the land at the deliverance of the princess, so much so that the prince determines to keep beside him this beneficent god, and not to permit him to return to Egypt; and indeed Khons remained three years and nine months in Bakhtan, and had no thought of returning to Thebes.

We must suppose that at the end of that period the god is seized with home-sickness, for one night, as the prince of Bakhtan was sleeping on his bed, he saw in a dream the god leaving his shrine in the form of a falcon of gold and flying skyward in the direction of Egypt The prince awoke sorely troubled; he summoned the priest of Khons and said: "The god desires to return to Egypt; let his chariot depart to that country." Needless to say, he did not let him depart without loading him with rich presents. The journey, like the first, lasted more than a year, and at the end of that time Khons-who-executes-plans entered

THE POSSESSED PRINCESS

his temple again safe and sound. He had the generosity to keep nothing for himself of all the presents made to him at Bakhtan, but to give everything up to Khons-Neferhotep.

In this last touch we may discover the motive in composing the tale. It seems clear that the statue or emblem of Khons was to be used in effecting miraculous cures. Khons would have to make other journeys besides the one to Bakhtan, though probably not so far afield; and the presents which never failed to be made to the god would be generously surrendered by him to the temple of the great god Khons-Neferhotep, which possessed an important and well-endowed college of priests. It is, indeed, hard not to believe that herein we have the aim and motive of the story, which is the product of a comparatively late time. It was, if I may be excused the familiar expression, a "puff" advertisement for the god Khons, whose cures were marvellous, like this one which was not so old, since it happened under the Rameses from whom the dynasty then in power had taken its name.

Khons-Neferhotep loved to mix in human affairs. An inscription of almost the same epoch as the foregoing tale supplies us with another example. It appears there had been some embezzlement going on in the temple of Amon, to such an extent that the festivals of the god had to be interrupted. A majordomo named Thothmes was gravely compromised, and the high priest of Amon, Pinodjem, was particularly anxious to clear him of the charge laid against him. For this purpose he applied to Khons-Neferhotep, the third member of the Theban triad. When this god was intended to give a sign, he was deposited in a part of the temple where there was a silver pavement. I can easily believe that it was a place where some mechanism was arranged for the purpose of making the limbs of the statue move, and that this mechanism was concealed by a metal floor. When the high priest arrived, the god nodded vigorously, and during the whole interview the god never stopped making signs of approval; he did even more. Pinodjem laid before him two writings, probably two scrolls, one of which bore the words: " It is said that there are matters which should be investigated in the case of Thothmes," and the other, words to the contrary effect.

Twice over Pinodjem displays the documents before Khons, who takes the latter and rejects the former; and the god thus declares by this choice that he abandons the accusation against the superintendent. But that is not enough. Thothmes appeared also before Amon, and the god not only remits the penalty of death which he had deserved, and all fines and punishment which he should have incurred, but he also makes it known by signs that Thothmes should be created " divine father," chief overseer of the granaries, accountant, chief guardian, and first inspector. And so the official who was supposed to be unfaithful is not only wholly exculpated, but promoted to far higher dignities than those he had formerly enjoyed. This shows us the purpose served by these statues thus endowed with movement or even with speech; and we can well understand that the priests made a diligent use of this means of persuasion in imposing on the credulity of the crowd.

I have dwelt at some length on the myths and on the use to which the priests put vocal or moving statues, because it appears to me that much light is thereby thrown on the religion of the people, as distinguished from the beliefs of the priests and the doctrines, more or less mysterious, recorded in the books whose composition was attributed to Thoth. In the myths and the statues we seem to grasp the conceptions which the common crowd formed of divinity and the influence which the deity had on their lives. The fellah of the time of Cheops or of Rameses worshipped above all the god of his own city, the deity whose sanctuary he saw at his door.

That deity might be called Horus in one place, Amon or Hathor in another; it might assume various forms; it had one or more sons; or it had created other deities. The great god of the temple, or one of the secondary deities sprung from him, was, in the eyes of the peasant, the incarnation of the forces or the phenomena of nature, especially the sun, the soil, and the Nile, on which his life depended. Now this belief was not forced on the people because there was a single form of religion in the country, but because all Egyptians lived under absolutely the same conditions, physical and climatic, and consequently were led to form a conception of divinity alike in all respects, whatever part of the country they lived in. The cosmic gods—those beings that were far off from them—did not satisfy them: they required to have gods brought nearer to them, and surrounded by conditions more akin to those in which they themselves lived,—in a word, they needed more human gods. Besides, they had arrived at the stage of making for themselves gods wholly anthropomorphic in their nature, or even able to assume the forms of the animals they saw every day around them. Hence arose these myths, in which the gods not only speak and act like human beings, but are also liable to the same weaknesses as men, and to quite mundane mishaps which they cannot avoid. These myths tell us that a god might be sometimes a falcon of gold or a black pig, or a cow supporting thousands of stars. The gods were also represented by small figures or statuettes which it was good to have at home, for they could preserve you from the bites of serpents or the stings of scorpions, without mentioning other means they possessed of exercising their protection over the inhabitants of the house.

Such, it appears to us, is the religion of the poor and obscure man: not the religion of the rich with his sumptuous funeral and magnificent tomb, but of the peasant or the artisan, whose body, when mummified, was thrown into the common trench. It is a nature-cult; above all, it is the worship of the Sun and the Nile, the two elements which fructified the third, the Earth, and brought life to human beings, and which, for everyday existence, assumed all terrestrial forms. As to knowing whether these three gods were one, or whether they were three emanations or creations of one and the same person—this was a question which the Egyptian of the common herd found it needless to put, and to which he was probably incapable of giving an answer.

VI

THE king did not become a god only after death when his body was shut up in a pyramid or hidden away in the depths of a rock-hewn tomb; he was divine all his life, in every act he performed — in war when he routed his enemies, as well as in peace when he laid the foundations of a temple. From his very birth he was a divine being: it was Amon who had given him life at the first; the god himself was his real father. The divine parentage of the sovereign is narrated for us in detail in the case of two monarchs of the eighteenth dynasty—the queen whose popular name is Hatasou, and King Amenhotep III. In both instances the whole legend is unfolded for us on the walls of the temples of Dér el

Bahri and Luqsor. Although it is first made known to us at this epoch—that is, at the most brilliant period of Egyptian history—I have no doubt, however, that the legend goes back much further; and it was kept up till a very late age, not only in the case of the kings, but of the gods themselves, for we find it again in the temple of Esneh, which dates from Roman times.

The following is an analysis of the most complete version we possess—that of the temple of Dér el Bahri. It deals, not with the birth of a king, but of a princess, who, from the fact that her husband, Thothmes II., died young, and owing also to her nephew, Thothmes III., being associated with her while he was still a child, held the sovereign power entirely in her own hands, and was not simply queen, but king—for she has herself always represented as a man. The legend opens with an assembly of the gods: Amon, the great god of Thebes, convenes all the great gods, and announces to them that he will beget a princess who will eclipse all the sovereigns who have been before her. Then Thoth, the Egyptian Hermes, conducts Amon to the queen. He names her to Amon, telling him that she is called Aahmes, and that she is more beautiful than any woman. Amon visits the queen, and finds her asleep. The scene that follows shows us Amon making the queen breathe the sign of life. Then he summons Khnoum, the potter, and commands him to fashion on his wheel the body of the princess and that of her double; and after that we see Queen Aahmes, who has just given birth to the princess, holding the child on her knees; the goddess Hathor will suckle her herself, and the sacred cows will take care of her doubles. There is, then, no doubt that the princess is a divine being; it is not Thothmes I., but Amon, who is her father. Henceforth her divine birth will be reflected in her whole existence; and, like her, the kings who come after will love to recall their origin by a picture, often found in

[*To face page* 266.

[*Photo by Translator*

The Hathor Cow, after removal from Shrine, February 1906.
The King, Amenhotep II., being suckled by the Cow.

the temples, of their being suckled by a goddess.

Following the nativity, we have the enthronement of the son of the gods by the gods themselves. They had to fulfil all the promises made to the child: an eternal sovereignty is predicted for him; they must now place him on the throne, and he, in his own person, must assume the duties which are the counterpart of the divine favours. The duties in which Amon, Ptah, or Ra take an interest are naturally those which concern themselves and their temples. The ritual of enthronement is made up of a succession of ceremonies: first, the purification and the presentation of the royal child to the gods, and it must be allowed that in all these ceremonies the gods themselves officiate. All the elaborate ritual depicted for us in the temple sculptures is really carried through; it is no make-believe. The gods are priests dressed up in the costume, the headgear, and the insignia of the various deities. The distinctive mark they assume is generally the head alone; but in some cases a more complete disguise was resorted to, as, for example, when the grotesque dwarf named Bes, or the goddess Api, who had a hippopotamus body, was represented. All this presupposes great credulity on the part of the Egyptians, but, at the same time, profound veneration for the divine element, since even such a travesty was sufficient to inspire a holy awe within them. It never entered the Egyptian mind to turn into ridicule a ceremony which, in certain respects, was only a masquerade: they knew how to look for and see the meaning that lay hidden under a show which sometimes must have been grotesque.

The purification was performed by two deities pouring water over the head of the king. At Dêr el Bahri it is Horus and Amon, and they say to the princess, " Thou art pure, and thy double also, in this solemn investiture of the King of Upper and of Lower Egypt "; after which naturally come promises of a long and happy life and of a reign without end. Then

PRESENTATION TO THE PEOPLE 269

she is presented to the gods; Amon takes her on his knees and embraces her; and next he shows her to the cycle of the gods of the South and the North.

When once the gods acknowledge her, the people who are to be her subjects must also see her and do homage. The ceremony is presided over by her father, the reigning king, who, being himself divine, plays the part of the god Ra. He is in a pavilion, with the prince (princess) whom he is about to associate with him in the government standing before him; then he takes his heir in his arms, in full view of the crowd, and places him on his throne. The assembly of the great officers of the kingdom prostrate themselves on the ground, and the king directs them, not only to be obedient and submissive henceforth to her whom he has just installed in his place, but even to worship her; "for my daughter has become divine, and the gods fight for her and are behind her every day to protect her, according to what the sovereign lord of the gods has decreed." Thus the father affirms formally before his assembled subjects the divine character of his heir—a character which necessitates paying the same honour to her as to the gods. Moreover, it is not a thing to surprise or shock his subjects to see a king worshipping himself, and taking a place among divinities to whom he renders divine honours, or even to range his bark in a temple-sanctuary side by side with those containing the emblems of the gods. Has he not been taught from childhood that he was a god, and has it not been publicly proclaimed in the hearing of the people of the kingdom? Is there anything, then, to prevent him from claiming on his own account the same privileges as other deities?

Amongst the company assembled to make the acquaintance of the princess, there is a class of priests charged with determining and proclaiming "the great name," or rather "the royal name." This name, which is, properly speaking, an entire sentence or paragraph, consists of different parts: first comes the name

DETERMINING THE ROYAL NAMES 271

of the *ka* or the double, of which we have already spoken in connection with the Thinite kings, and which determines that the king is a Horus, that is, that he belongs to the old conquering race whose standard was a falcon. This falcon is perched on a dwarfed representation of the door of a tomb through which the deceased's double passes in and out after his death. On the lintel of this door are some signs, which usually represent an epithet—forming the name of the double. In the case of Queen Hatasou, her *ka* name is "She who is rich in *kas*, or powerful through her *kas*"; her father's was "The powerful Bull beloved of Maat, the goddess of Truth or Justice." After the *ka* name, which is often called the standard or banner name, comes a second epithet, introduced by these words, "Lord of the two crowns," that is, those of the East and of the West. The Queen's second epithet is

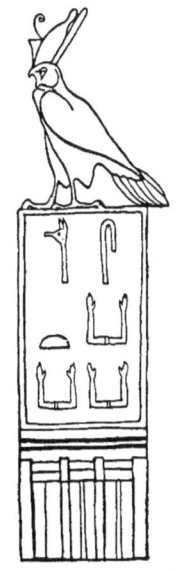

Horus name of Queen Hatasou, "rich in *kas*."

"Abounding in years," or sometimes "She who takes possession of all lands"; her father's corresponding title was "He who rises like a flame, the very courageous." This part of the name was not absolutely fixed, but capable of variations, like the third part of the name, which is always introduced by the group "The Golden Horus." Here again, in the case of the Queen, we have two different versions: "She who is divine in her risings," and "She who vivifies hearts." Her father had several Golden-Horus names, one of which was "He who smites the barbarians."

After these came the royal title properly so-called: it serves usually to designate the person of the sovereign, "the King of Upper and of Lower Egypt," followed by two cartouches separated by the words "Son of Ra." A cartouche is an oval enclosing a certain number of signs forming the name of the king. The cartouches are generally two in number, the first of which is the name given at the enthronement, and always contains the word

Ra, the Sun; it is the solar prenomen, the one that connects the prince with the great god. That of Hatasou means "the true double (*ka*) (the true image) of Ra." After the words "Son of Ra" comes the second cartouche, containing the ordinary name of the king which he received at birth. We now give the complete style of the Queen, which would be inscribed on the monuments: " The Horus, powerful through his *kas*, lord of the two crowns who abounds in years, the Golden Horus who vivifies hearts, the King of Upper and of Lower Egypt, Ka-ma-Ra (true *ka* of Ra), Son of the Sun, Hatshepsut Khnoumit Amon (Hatshepsut joined to Amon)." We thus see that the divine character of the king or queen distinctly stands out in this protocol, which is duly proclaimed, and, we should say, registered by the priests assembled on the occasion.

After the king or the queen has received these names, various ceremonies complete the coronation, the most important being that in which the queen is conducted into two pavilions where there are gods who place on her head successively the diadem of the South and that of the North. Then the monarch goes round a walled enclosure, called the Northern Hall, near the hall in which he received the crowns. He is accompanied in this round by the great god of the locality, who embraces him, thereby transmitting to him authority over the whole land and over the territories belonging to the Nine Bows or the Barbarians. Throughout the ceremony the gods always treat the king like one of themselves; they assert and consecrate his divine character, but it is not wholly gratuitously. He must acknowledge it in some way, and do what is pleasing to them. He enters into obligations towards them which he will have to fulfil, as Horemheb, the last sovereign of the eighteenth dynasty, did, of whom it is said: "From the day the king took possession of this land he reorganised it as it was in the time of the god Ra. He restored the temples of the gods;

he renewed all their divine statues in greater number than they had been before; . . . what the king found in ruins, he set up again in its place. He made one hundred statues life-size, of costly stone. He visited all the cities where the gods had buildings, in all this land, and endowed them just as they had been at the beginning, and he established for them all their daily offerings, and all the vessels necessary for their buildings, wrought in gold and in silver; he equipped them with priests, officiating ministers, and picked soldiers; he made gifts to them in writing of fields and cattle, and supplied them with everything that it was meet for them to have." This was the way in which the gods asked to be recompensed.

If the matter in hand was the founding of a building, say a temple, it was carried out with the co-operation of the gods; the ceremonies were regulated by a book called "The Book of the Foundation of Temples for the Gods of the First Ennead." The work was begun at night, so that the king might determine the axis of the temple by the stars. He took four stakes, and a surveying line or cord, and first marked out the four corners of the building. He was assisted in this operation by a goddess Safekhaboui or Seshaït, "She who watched over the house of the books,"—the divine keeper of the records—she who also wrote on a palm-branch or on the fruit of the sacred tree the years of the king. The four corners marked out, the king then provided himself with a hoe, with which he traced the boundary of the temple; then he marked its outline by pouring out some sand on it, which made the marks stand out on the black soil. Then he moulded a brick for each of the four corners of the building, but under one of the corners he placed the foundation deposits which are often found in the excavations. Although the texts inform us that these deposits "are bricks of gold and precious stones for the corners of the temple," it is seldom that this statement is completely corroborated by the discoveries made in our

FOUNDING OF A TEMPLE

time. The foundation deposits often consist of small plaques of gold or of enamel bearing the name of the king who founded the temple, but, for the most part, however, they are simply small models of the tools used in the construction. Then the king lays the first stone, which he pushes with a lever into its place. At this point, probably before the laying of the stone, a sacrifice had to be made: the only one that we meet with is that of a decapitated bird; but we may admit that here we have the mild survival of a very ancient practice, found among other nations, which required that the laying of the first stone should be sprinkled with human blood.

It appears that upon the occasion of the building the king had a small model of a house or a pylon made; and then came the question of consecrating it to the god. For this purpose the king scattered various kinds of incense round about, and when he was offering it to the god, he changed the model into a divine thing by touching it with his mace a certain number of times. At the laying of a foundation stone, we have almost invariably a scene presented to us which is by no means clear in its meaning. The king holds in one hand an oar, and in the other a tool or instrument which looks like a mason's square; he is making a great stride, as if in the act of running. As a companion picture to this we have generally another scene quite similar: the king making the same stride, but holding now a libation vase in each hand. M. Moret, to whom we owe a learned study of all the rites, from which we have borrowed much, regards these scenes as a consecration, the water of the vases and the fire of the solar emblems symbolising the purification of the structure. I rather think that the striding or running takes place quite at the beginning of the foundation ceremony, and that the king is stepping out the site on which the building is to be erected, and of which he wishes to make a gift to the gods. Be that as it may, the king in all these ceremonies is acting as a divine being; he is the son of Amon, to whom he dedicates the temple, and it is as a son paying the homage due to a father that he himself handles the tool which will be used in the construction of the building.

Besides the coronation, there were other great festivals in which divine honours were paid to the king. One of them in particular, called the *Sed* festival, often supposed to be the anniversary of the king's accession to the throne, was usually celebrated at an interval of about thirty years. I consider the *Sed* period as being fiscal in its nature, and its inaugural festival as an indiction date—that is, the date on which the taxes and dues leviable on the inhabitants of the country were imposed for a stated number of years; and since the foundation of every impost was the tenth or tithe—that is, the amount paid for worship and everything connected with it—there is nothing surprising in the fact that the Festival of the Indiction had a specially religious character. As such we already find it represented on the monuments of the Thinite epoch; and it continued to be so down to the Roman period.

At this festival the king comes out of an apartment, reserved for him in the temple, called the sanctuary; then he ascends into a pavilion open at the four sides, with four staircases leading up to it. Carrying the emblems of Osiris in his hands, he takes his seat on a throne, and turns to the four cardinal points, one after the other; each time he does this, two gods or goddesses raise their hands above his head and repeat at each of the four times, " The South is united to the North," or " The heavens are joined to the earth." It is a kind of second enthronement. Then the king presents himself before the principal deity of the temple. During his progress he is escorted by the genii of the South and the North, who sometimes even carry him in a palanquin. On the threshold of the hall where the god whom he is going to visit resides, a deity makes him a libation of welcome. The god embraces him. Thoth and Safekhaboui draw up in writing the record of the festival, determine for him an infinite number of years of reign, or inscribe his name on the fruit of the sacred tree of Heliopolis.

On leaving that hall he passes into the banqueting-room, where may be seen several pavilions each containing a statue of a god, before whom are heaped up all kinds of offerings and victuals. Not seldom the statue of the king himself stands among the other statues; and sometimes the king acts as a priest making offerings to himself. This last act may be regarded as the climax of the deification of the king. He is so much a god, he partakes to such an extent in the divine nature, he is deemed to possess so completely the power and the privileges of divinity, that he does not hesitate to worship himself, to make offerings to himself, and above all to take his place among the gods to whom other priests besides himself offer worship.

This fact has often been regarded as a proof of the haughty presumption characteristic of Rameses II. When, for instance, at Abu

Simbel we see his statue at the far end of the sanctuary, along with three of the great gods of Egypt; or when we read his name on the bas-reliefs alongside of the deities to whom he is offering wine or milk, we are apt to think, at first sight, that this was a personal freak of his, an exhibition of a mania for greatness on his part pushed to an extreme. Nothing of the kind: Rameses II. was by no means the only one of the kings of Egypt to whom worship was given. There is no presumption in all this, nor any trace of impiety, on his part. This procedure was perfectly legitimate; it was but the outcome of the conception which the Egyptians formed of the king. and was accepted by universal consent. Begotten by a god, suckled by goddesses, and receiving at their hands at his coronation all the privileges and attributes of divinity, the king is one of themselves, he belongs to their cycle, and he can lay claim, as well as they, to the honours paid to them. In the great temples there was usually a bark in which stood a tabernacle containing the emblem of the god of the locality: the king had also his bark containing his emblem. This emblem, I believe, was a fan, one of the symbols of the double, which also represents the royal person in the processions where we see it placed on a throne.

The real distinction between the king and ordinary mortals is this: they become gods only after death, by assimilation to or fusion with Osiris; he, on the other hand, is a god all his life, he is so from birth; consequently, during all his life he can lay claim to have divine worship paid to him, over and above the great festivals and special ceremonies which bring his divine nature into special relief. We can show, as we have already seen, the existence of a regular cult of the sovereign in the sculptures on the temple of Dér el Bahri. There we find a chamber which was specially consecrated to the queen, and which was dedicated to her in her lifetime. She sits there before an altar, while a long procession of priests bring offerings of all kinds to her;

and on the walls of the room are engraved certain chapters from the Pyramid Texts. The whole seems to bear a close resemblance to a funerary service or cult; and in the chamber beside the queen's, which is dedicated to the deceased Thothmes I., we see representations which are almost identical. In this case, however, there is no possible doubt that the cult is paid to a dead man. But, in the case of the queen's chamber, it is quite otherwise: she was still full of life when this chamber was decorated; she had still many years of rule before her. Now, as we can hardly suppose that she had all the details of the cult that was to be paid to her later, executed and painted in advance, we must admit that already in her lifetime these acts of divine homage were paid to her as to a divine being. After her death the cult would continue; nothing would be changed; there would be the same priests, the same offerings, the same religious and magical formulæ. And this consideration leads me to adopt a different conclusion from M. Moret's: I believe that the cult of dead kings was only the continuation of what was accorded them in their lifetime. In my opinion the gods were not at first dead; on the contrary, I believe they were at first living, on whose behalf was continued to be paid, perhaps in a modified or a developed form, the cult or service they enjoyed during their life.

Besides the cult of the king, there was another which was addressed to the numerous divinities of the Pantheon, with a complicated ritual of its own which necessitated a large number of various offices. We know this from the temple of Abydos, where there is a record engraved on the walls of seven chambers, each consecrated to a different deity. These texts were reproduced on papyri which have come down to us. Scattered fragments of the ritual are also to be met with on the temple walls of every epoch. They give us the daily service done by the service priest, or, as he was called in Egyptian, "in his day," as the king's substitute, for theoretically the king alone was worthy to appear before the gods and to discharge the sacred offices. But as it was obviously impossible for him to do this in all the temples of the land, or even to tie himself down to the very strict duties which the cult of a single deity involved, he had of course to delegate the duty to a priest who became his substitute. Yet the original idea that the priesthood belonged essentially to the king persisted to the latest times. In the numberless pictures we have of religious acts performed before a god, it is always the king who is supposed to do it. The thought may also have been present that there was no better means of honouring the god than by showing that the only personage worthy of serving him was his descendant, his son, he who was of the same race as himself, and his equal.

The ritual of Abydos—the same as that of Thebes—refers to statues of gilt-wood, incrusted with precious stones. They were placed in a *naos*, or a tabernacle of wood or stone, which the officiating priest alone had the right of opening. It is thus but a portion of the ceremonial that is contained in this ritual. The gods were not always statues; some of them were represented by emblems like a sistrum, or an animal like a falcon. Rules and prescriptions existed for the ceremonies performed in their honour, as well as for all those ceremonies which took place outside the temples, such as carrying the sacred boat with its *naos* from place to place. The ritual we possess is the ritual observed in the cult of the statues celebrated within the temple. The title of the book on a papyrus is, "The beginning of the chapters of the divine rites done in the temple of Amon Ra, king of the gods, in the course of every day, by the high priest of the service." The cult of the statue included precise gestures, accompanied by formulæ which are often very obscure; they explain to us what the priest has to do, and subjoin magical phrases or allusions to myths of which we have only an imperfect knowledge.

The priest is in the sanctuary; the tabernacle is still closed; he must begin with purifications, by fire, by fumigation, and by water. He kindles a fire, chiefly to light up the hall, which otherwise would be in complete darkness; then he takes the censer, places the bowl for burning the incense on the censer, and sprinkles some grains of incense on the flame and advances towards the holy place. Each of these acts is accompanied by formulæ in which the priest from the outset poses as a god; but he is not alone in this respect, for each of the articles he uses has a divine "name"—that is, it has a divine personality, and is addressed as a divinity. Here, for instance, is what is said to the censer: "Homage to thee, O censer of the gods who are of the following of Thoth: my two arms are upon thee, like those of Horus; my two hands are upon thee, like those of Thoth; my fingers are upon thee, like those of Anubis,

THE DAILY SERVICE

chief of the divine shrine: I am the living slave of Ra; I am pure, for I have purified myself, and my purifications are the purifications of the gods." These words, spoken to the censer, are the same which will be addressed to Amon himself. The divine nature is thus like an emanation, an effluent, which is transmitted from the god to the officiating priest, and from him to all the objects he touches and uses.

The second act of the ritual is the entry of the priest into the *naos*, where he must purify the statue and take it in his arms. He breaks the seal, removing the clay sealing, for the *naos* was tightly closed; then he slips back the bolt—or, as the text calls it, "the finger of Set"—and finds himself in presence of the statue. The statue is covered, according to an interpretation which I think may be given to a slightly ambiguous phrase, with an animal's skin, which he begins to remove; the face of the god is thus unveiled, and the priest can behold him. To see a god, or rather to look at him, is a privilege granted only to a king, or to his deputy, a priest; and the act is not without danger, either to the beholder or even to the god, since the look or glance which falls on him is that of a king—that is, a god. The power of the eye is acknowledged —a power which may often be formidable and even destructive, as the speech of the officiating priest testifies: "My face is preserved from the god; the god is preserved from my divine face; for it is the gods who have made for me the road whereon I walk, and it is the king who has sent me to behold the god." Thus neither of the two runs any risk. Next, the priest bows low to the ground— literally "smells the ground"—and then lies flat on his stomach. Each of his acts is accompanied by words like these: "Homage to thee, Amon Ra! Thou art well established in thy great dwelling. I have lain down on my stomach out of dread of thee, for I experience fear before the terror which thou dost inspire; I embrace Keb and Hathor, so that I may be strong and that I may not fall a victim of the sacrifices of this day." Then he rises up, while uttering other words. All this is much the same as what occurs in mosques at the hour of prayer; from time to time, while he repeats the words, the devotee prostrates himself and touches the ground with his forehead; then he recovers himself; again, he raises his arms. There is this difference: he has no statue before him, like the Egyptian priest.

When the latter regains his feet he utters a hymn in praise of the god: " Homage to thee, Amon Ra, Lord of Thebes, the young man who is the ornament of the gods! All men rejoice at sight of thee—him who is the lord of terror, who calms fear, the prince of all the gods, the great living god, the well-beloved who pleases the gods by his words, king of the sky, the creator of the stars, the gold of the gods who traverses the horizon and who calls the gods into being when he speaks. . . . Amon Ra, the lord of the beams of light, the creator of the hosts, the god of the uplifted plumes, the king of the gods. . . ."

He next proceeds to make the offerings and the fumigations, and presents the statue with a perfume made of honey, followed by incense. Finally, the priest embraces the statue: in a real embrace, not difficult to do, since the limbs of the statue are jointed; after this the priest retires for the first time. Entering again, he makes the same gestures, prostrates himself again, chants fresh hymns in honour of the god, and offers a small figure representing the goddess Maat. She is the goddess of Justice, Truth, and Law; and it appears to me that, in offering this emblem to a god, he who presents the offering gives the god to understand that he grants him the right of imposing law on him, and that he will regard the god henceforth as his judge, to whose decrees and pleasure he is ready to submit. It is, in my opinion, a means of rendering homage to the god, of declaring that he, the offerer, recognises the god as his lord and

[*To face page* 292.

[*Photo by Translator*

Sety I. offering Maat (Truth) to Osiris, Abydos.

master: the emblem of the goddess is but the pledge of the act of submission. So this offering of the image of Maat is always amongst the first made, very soon after entering.

The statue must now be dressed in full. But first it has to submit to sundry washings with water contained in various vases; then more incense is burnt again to it; and after that the god's clothes are put on. First two white fillets are given him for wrapping round his head; these bandlets are rolled up; after which the same thing is done with a green-coloured bandlet, and a third one of red. Then the body of the deity is wrapped round with a piece of stuff, and different kinds of face-paint or perfumes, the nature of which we do not exactly know, are given to him. Each of these offerings is accompanied by symbolical or magical formulæ, in which occur allusions which in many cases we do not understand. Moreover, it is the characteristic of every magical expression to be unintelligible: without that quality it would certainly lose its efficacy. After several more purifications, the ceremony is at an end; the priest comes out of the shrine, the door is shut close, and a seal is affixed to it.

Such, briefly, is the complicated ceremonial, teeming with repetitions, and taking up so much time that we are tempted to ask if it could really be celebrated every day. M. Moret sees in all this ceremonial the cult of a defunct person paid to a mortal being who, like Ra, dies every day, and is exposed at all times to the attack of a typhonian god. The object of the cult in Egypt would then be the protection of the god from possible death, by performing over him the rites which availed to resuscitate Osiris and deceased persons. We have already stated above that it is, in our opinion, too sweeping an assertion to make, that every kind of Egyptian cult originated in the cult of the dead. It seems to us rather that the cult of the dead is, in a sense, the *prolongation* of the life—the desire to continue existence to the person who has left this world, and that under a form which was not always the same. During the Old Empire, men's thoughts ran on a life wholly like that of this world; later, they dreamt of a condition more nearly approaching that of divinity. It is impossible for us to recognise any system or coherency in this ritual, or any fructifying idea developing logically to a conclusion : we find, rather, a reflection of the most diverse conceptions which the Egyptians formed regarding the gods. Sometimes the god addressed by the priest may be regarded as an Osiris, that is, as a dead god who is to be resuscitated; at other times, he is quite alive, as, for instance, at the moment the priest enters the shrine, when a simple glance cast at him by the god might be fatal. The ritual is not, any more than the Book of the Dead, the expression of a single and well-defined conception of divinity.

Before leaving the ritual, one question remains to be put. What part did sacrifice play in the Egyptian cult; and, in particular, were there human sacrifices? One thing is certain: in the representations of the cult we very frequently see the slaughter of a bull or an antelope. The animal, whose throat has been cut, is lying on its side; its four legs are tied together; butchers are cutting it up, who begin by severing the forelegs, then the head; then they take out the heart, and lastly they remove the great hind-quarters. The numerous pictures where this is seen are almost identical; the first operation which the sculptors are fond of showing is the removal of one of the forelegs; but all this is a sacrifice solely because priests figure in the scene and do the work— the meaning of the operation is not essentially religious. The intention, above everything, is to procure for the god an offering to be laid on his altar; for all the pieces prepared, called "the choice parts," are brought to him by the priests. It is, however, probable that we have here a remote reminiscence of the death of enemies whose bodies, or spoils taken from them, were offered. Doubtless the idea of the offering—the food or nourishment—brought to the god, just as it is brought to the double, plays the principal part; nevertheless the original idea recurs again and again—for example, in the phrase of the official in bringing the heart, "I have brought thee the heart of thy enemy."

This offering is made not only to the gods but to the dead. For them, too, bulls, gazelles, and birds were immolated, being regarded as enemies; for, as M. Lefébure brings out, the object of this ceremony was the appropriation and absorption of the life of the victims by the recipient. This would necessarily imply that these victims were substitutes for human beings. Sometimes it was sufficient to offer the deceased the head of an ox; or, in other cases, the victim that was placed in the tomb was mummified, so that the effect of the sacrifice should have the same eternal duration as was desired for the body of the deceased.

We found in the myth of the Destruction

of Mankind what the priests of Thebes in the nineteenth dynasty regarded as the origin of sacrifices. When Ra, weary of the society of men, prepares to be raised to the sky by Nout, he still notices some men who had escaped the slaughter; and in the morning, when these men sally forth with their bows and arrows, and offer, as we suppose, to destroy his enemies, he replies: "Your sins are behind you (forgiven); slaughter averts slaughter, hence come sacrifices," as the text adds. This explanation does not define the kind of sacrifices instituted on this occasion; but the logical conclusion to be drawn from it is that human sacrifices are in question. If the death of the enemies of Ra avails to pardon men for rebelling against their king —if this death has an expiatory value—it would seem that it should be the death of a being the equal of him who thus escapes condemnation, and not the death of a mere ox or a gazelle substituted for him—at least so long as these animals are not regarded as

HUMAN SACRIFICE IN EGYPT 299

forms of Set, the enemy of Osiris. We know that Set often assumes the forms of animals; but as this god is not named in the myth of the Destruction of Mankind, we cannot accept this explanation as satisfactory.

There is, indeed, in the Egyptian texts a reminiscence of human sacrifices; there is even more. A king of the eighteenth dynasty, Amenhotep II., returning from Syria, recounts the following: " His Majesty returned with joy of heart to his father Amon, and slew with his own mace the seven princes." M. Lefébure sees in this barbarous act a sacrifice. It seems to me that here we have rather an example of a custom widely prevalent in other countries as well as in Egypt, of putting the chiefs of conquered enemies to death; and not only conquered foes, but every class of foreigner, who was instinctively regarded as an enemy. This feeling is also shown even in our own day amongst uncivilised peoples. Several Greek authors tell us how the Egyptians sacrificed strangers; but Herodotus mentions this only to contradict it, and he informs us that the Egyptians offer in sacrifice only swine, geese, sheep, bulls, or calves (such of them as are clean), and he asks, "How should they, then, sacrifice human beings?"

There exists in a Theban tomb a series of very strange representations of an almost unique

Man in Skin on Sledge.

(From Tomb of *Paheri* (eighteenth dynasty) at El Kab)

kind. The subject is a funerary rite, celebrated in honour of a great personage, who was not, however, of royal race, and could not therefore claim special honours. We see him seated on a stool; before him two priests are digging a pit in the ground; then he stands up and looks at four servants dragging a man who is lying on a hurdle, face downwards; a fifth

HUMAN SACRIFICE IN EGYPT 301

servant spreads out a large hide. The man lying down is called *Teken*, or, following M. Maspero's vocalisation, *Tikanou*. Another tomb shows us the man wrapped up in the skin, lying on a sort of stool, with face still turned earthwards. I am inclined to see in this ceremony, as M. Maspero does, a symbol of the new birth. The man passes through the skin of an animal, and this brings him to life again, in the same way that we have seen the sun passing through a gigantic serpent in the Twelfth Hour in order to be born again. I cannot think that the *Tikanou* is sacrificed, for in the same scene we see a sacrificer taking off the heads of a cow and a gazelle, and this does not happen to the man lying on the hurdle.

Further on, the sledge reappears, carried on the shoulders of two men who, it is said, are going to throw it into the place of destruction; and, as a matter of fact, we see a sledge in the hole that has been dug in the ground. Quite at the side two men are lying, face downwards, on the ground; they are swathed up and support themselves merely by their hands. The text calls them Nubians, Anou, the people who in our opinion were the primitive African population of Egypt. If now we refer to the oldest documents which have been preserved—those of the Thinite epoch—we find it mentioned once: " the bringing of the heads of the Anou into the sanctuary "; there is also a festival which was continued in later times, called " the festival of the smiting of the Anou." It is indisputable that there are in the picture we are discussing the remains of a very old tradition; and it appears, indeed, that in former days they resorted on great occasions to human sacrifices, when the victims were those vanquished people over whom the Horites had established their sway.

But to return to the Nubians in the tomb. A little further on we see them unswathed and on their knees between two officials who have put a rope round their necks and appear to strangle them. Above the heads of the

[To face page 302.

Man in Skin on Sledge. [Photo by Translator.

(From Renni's Tomb, El Kab.)

Nubians we see the crenelated enclosure which is the sign of foreign peoples, and in a cartouche two characters which read *Kesui*, a word of various meanings. Here, I think, it ought to be translated " the two swathed ones," that is, the personages who, a little before, are seen lying face downwards, without a sign of motion. We shall find, a little further on, the same crenelated cartouche with characters which read " black hairs"; also, a ditch or trench into which have been thrown the hide of the *Tikanou*, the hair, the leg, and the heart of the cows sacrificed, in order to be burned. All this leads me to think that the question here is not that of a real human sacrifice, but a fictitious or sham sacrifice. Indeed, I do not believe that the *Tikanou* and the Nubians were men whom they would readily subject to such a fiction. I believe that the swathed figures were puppets or lay figures which they made a show of strangling before they were thrown into the hole, to be destroyed by fire. On this point I am not able to agree with M. Maspero; I do not believe that they were made to submit to this treatment in order to send to the dead man slaves or companions to wait on him in the next world. The *ushabti* figures answered this end; thousands of them could be laid in the tombs; it would be enough even if they were represented on the walls. These puppets had formerly been enemies; what, therefore, was required was not the perpetuation of their life, but, on the contrary, some action which would ensure the destruction of their double and prevent it from coming into conflict with that of the deceased. Here, then, as on so many other occasions, the sacrifice recalls and commemorates a victory of long ago.

Yet it appears to me very probable that this sacrifice in the tomb we are speaking of is only a fictitious ceremony. The strangling of the Nubians here is in the same category as the clubbing by the king, at a single blow, of a bunch of enemies whom he holds by the

COUNTERFEIT SACRIFICE 305

hair of the head: both are symbolic represcutations. I do not pretend to say that the Egyptians did not sacrifice human victims on certain solemn occasions, as, for instance, at a time of national calamity; this was the case

Man in Skin. [Photo by Translator.]
(From Sen-nofer's Tomb at Thebes.)

among all nations of antiquity: and no doubt, also, at the beginning, human sacrifice accompanied festivals held for the celebration of brilliant triumphs. But in later times the human victim was replaced by animals. We have proof of this in an Edfou inscription of the Ptolemaic epoch. It describes a solemn festival held to commemorate the victories of Horus. We are told that his victories are accomplished, that he has smitten to the death all enemies, even the Asiatics; and in remembrance there is brought forth, not a

[Photo by Translator.

Man in Skin. Man in Skin.
(From Tomb of Menna at Thebes.)

human being, but a hippopotamus, and not a live one either, but one of paste or dough, to be sacrificed, and we see a sacrificing priest plunging his knife into the hide of the creature! And so, since they had reached the point of giving up even animal sacrifice and of being content with an artificial victim,

A PTOLEMAIC FICTION 307

they had all the stronger reason for abandoning the practice of human sacrifice, at least in the customary worship, which was regulated by rules that were put in force every day.

No doubt it is sometimes dangerous to build on the absence of a representation of any one fact in order to conclude therefrom the non-existence of the fact itself; yet in the case before us it would be extraordinary, if human sacrifices had really existed—if they had formed part of the usual rites,—not to find a single instance of them among the innumerable religious pictures which adorn the temple walls. The only one met with up to the present day is that which I have just described, and assuredly it is difficult to regard it as being very conclusive.

If now we cast a glance over the Egyptian religion, we perceive that what appears to be its dominant feature, especially in later times, is its wealth of ceremonies, and the pomp and splendour of its manifestations. It certainly held a large place in the life of the nation. Its great festivals, continually recurring; its ritual, so complex in its nature; the innumerable statues of deities whose names and attributes are incessantly changing—all this must make a great impression on the visitor who sets his foot in the country for the first time; and when we add to this the mysterious language used by the priests in the ceremonies, the magic power to which they laid claim, with results apparently analogous to those which Indian travellers tell us of at the present day, we shall understand how the Egyptians had acquired, outside their own country, a reputation for wisdom and knowledge such as had no parallel in any other nation. This reputation, too, must have had a real foundation before such lofty spirits as Solon, Pythagoras, and Plato deemed it incumbent on them to come personally to imbibe this knowledge, and to undertake the journey at a time when certainly the country was in decadence, and when the meaning of the religious books, and especially of the symbolism, was probably perishing rapidly.

In the Greek period, under the Macedonian kings, it was the entirely external side of the cult that predominated. The ceremonies and the ritual which had already, in the nineteenth dynasty, grown so rich and exuberant at Abydos and Thebes, now became much more so under the Ptolemies. These kings, as well as the Romans, knew well that the best means of securing their sway over the country was to constitute themselves protectors of its religion, and to be benefactors of the temples and of everything pertaining to the cult. It was the period when the beautiful temples of Denderah, Edfou, Ombos, and Philæ, which have survived to this day, were built. And they are all constructed on one regular plan, the original of which can be traced back to ancient times, to the days of Cheops, the builder of the Great Pyramid, or even to the time of " the followers of Horus," the legendary predecessors of Mena. Several inscriptions inform us of considerable endowments bestowed on particular sanctuaries by the kings; and, in return, the grateful priests willingly devoted themselves to institute and regulate the cults of those kings or queens who, like the old Pharaohs, gave out that they were of divine birth.

All this was only in harmony with the rules and customs inherited from the most distant ages, for the Ptolemies were no innovators, either in the civil sphere or, above all, in the religious domain.

Yet the inscriptions on these temples differ from those on the ancient edifices: they are, for one thing, infinitely fuller. When Thothmes III. or Sety I. had the walls of their temples decorated, they no doubt had religious scenes portrayed; but the inscription was brief—it simply indicated the nature of the rite or of the offering, to which were added promises, wearisomely repeated, made to the king by the god. At other times, longer texts relate some episode in the king's life, or a successful war; battle scenes, too, and prisoners brought back to Egypt are frequent subjects. But in the Ptolemaic structures there is nothing of all this, no historic scene: if there are wars, they are those which Horus waged with Set. To make up for this, however, there is a profusion of regulations and prescriptions of the most minute kind for everything pertaining to worship. Every chamber of the temple has its name, and its purpose is explained to us: if it happens to be a room for the vestments of the god or goddess, we are told what these vestments are made of; if it is the library, the books in it are mentioned; if it is the place where the drugs are prepared, we are told in detail how it is done; if it is a staircase which is used on a great festival day, the walls will show us the order of the priests in the procession; if it is the great Hall of Entrance, called the "Hall of the Sky," the ceiling will be a kind of celestial map, giving us the names of the day and the night hours.

A reason for this notable change has been alleged, namely, the fact that the knowledge of everything relating to religion was being gradually lost, and therefore it became necessary to fix in stone what was still known, for the instruction of future generations. I should rather believe that the change was due to a modification in the religion itself. It had lost its spiritual character and was now nothing but a thing of forms and ceremonies. And just in proportion as these forms and ceremonies increased in number, they always grew more detailed, and demanded an ever-increasing staff to perform them. The Ptolemaic tomb, again, is no longer the abode of the dead, to be decorated with a view to its occupatiou by the deceased in the life after death. The kings no more have funerary chapels built in connection with a tomb situated some distance off; and even religious books, properly so-called, like the Pyramid Texts or

EXCESSIVE DEVELOPMENT OF MAGIC 313

the Book of the Lower World, no longer appear to be sought after, with the exception of the Book of the Dead, of which often very incorrect copies are still met with, made by scribes who did not understand what they were writing. People are no longer concerned about them; such books are forgotten, except, however, those devoted to magic—a subject which was always dear to the Egyptian heart. To such a pitch was the devotion to magic carried, that in Rome the Egyptian religion was often regarded as nothing but sorcery, and its priests had an evil reputation. In the first centuries of the Christian era a fusion took place, above all in Egypt—for I do not speak here of any other country,—of Greek or Roman deities with the old Egyptian gods; and this mixture produced a crop of small terra-cotta figures, of which we possess a very large number, representing these Græcised Egyptian deities, each with a name sufficiently modified, so as to allow of its pronunciation by a Greek tongue. Thus we are acquainted with a crowd of forms of Harpocrates, who is none other than "Horus-the-child"; and as, childlike, he held his finger in his mouth, the Greeks took him for the God of Silence! Isis is often seen suckling her son; sometimes he is a serpent, as Osiris is too; and Horus is seen on horseback transfixing his enemies. In all these figures, what are called the old conventional forms have been abandoned; a freedom of treatment unknown to the old artists has come in; but the mixture is hardly happy, being neither Egyptian nor Greek, but a compound hybrid, the effect of which is seldom pleasing to behold. Other elements are also introduced, from the Semitic world. Traces of Semitic influence are found on the stones that were used as amulets; in fact, all the superstitions of foreign lands, and all charms and magic arts seem to have been concentrated in Egypt.

But in a short time Christianity made itself felt. It was not established without violence, for fanatical iconoclasts like Shenouti and

St Macaire spread destruction among the religious edifices of old Egypt. But the Egyptian spirit survived many a long day, as, for example, in the mode of burial. I found in the temple of Dér el Bahri mummies which were undoubtedly Christian. On the linen in which they were wrapped might be seen the cup, the ear of corn, the bread and the wine, the symbols of the Last Supper, side by side with other emblems derived from the religion of the old Pharaohs. And Gnosticism, which plays so great a part in Christian Egypt, is certainly a product of the old religious conceptions.

The latest books which reflect the beliefs of old Egypt are those attributed to Hermes Trismegistus, and hence called the Hermetic Books. They have long enjoyed high authority. They consist of different fragments written in Greek, fourteen of which have been collected under the title of Poimandres; others are cited by the scholiasts or the fathers, Stobæus, Cyril, Lactantius, and Suidas; lastly, there is a dialogue called Asclepius, which we know only through a Latin translation erroneously attributed to Apuleius. M. Ménard, to whom we owe a brilliant study and a translation of these books, regards them as the sole surviving monuments known of the Egyptian philosophy, although they only appear in Greek. It is true that here and there in the doctrine we find a great analogy between it and the doctrines revealed in portions of the old literature: we read, for instance, that God is the universal life, the All of whom individual beings are but parts, "God is all, everything is full of him; there is nothing in the universe that is not God. All names meet in him as the father of the universe." Or again: "Everything is a part of God; so God is all; in creating he creates himself." If we substitute for "God" the old expression "this God," that is, Amon, we fancy we are reading a fragment of a hymn composed in the time of Rameses II. That there are present in the Hermetic Books Jewish and even Christian

THE HERMETIC BOOKS 317

influences, no one can deny. There are, however, portions which appear to have been written by an adept in the old religion—one of these men who, to the very last, tried to maintain the beliefs and the ceremonies of the old priests, in certain remote spots like the Island of Philæ, where the Egyptian cult survived to the days of the Emperor Theodosius (379–395 A.D.). The author of the discourse named Asclepius, which we know only in a Latin translation, is one of these last faithful souls whom nothing could shake; and in words of true eloquence he takes a prophetic farewell of that religion which had endured for more than four thousand years, and whose destruction would be the forerunner of terrible calamities that would smite the whole world.

"Yet, as wise men ought to foresee all events, it is a thing which you must know: a time will come when it will seem as if the Egyptians had all in vain fulfilled the worship of the gods with so much piety, and as if all their holy invocations had been barren and unheard. The divinity will abandon the earth and will ascend again to the heavens, utterly forsaking Egypt his ancient abode, and leaving her widowed of religion, bereft of the presence of the gods. With foreigners filling the heavens and the earth, not only will all holy things be neglected, but, what is harder still, religion, piety, worship of the gods will be proscribed and punished by law. Then this land, made sacred by so many shrines and temples, will be covered with tombs and the dead. O Egypt! Egypt! there will remain to thee nothing of thy religions but vague tales which after ages will not believe; nothing but words graven on stone, telling of thy piety. The Scythian or the Indian, or some other barbarian neighbour, will inhabit Egypt. The Divine One will ascend to the heavens again, and humanity abandoned will die completely out, and Egypt will be a desert, and widowed of men and gods.

"I address myself to thee, O most holy Stream, and I foretell thy future. Tides of blood, polluting thy divine waves, will overflow thy banks; the number of the dead will exceed that of the living; and if any inhabitants remain, they will be Egyptian only in their speech, but they will be foreigners in their ways. Dost thou weep, Asclepius? There will be things sadder still. Egypt herself will fall into apostasy, the depth of evils. She, in other days the Sacred Land, beloved of the gods for her devotion to their service, will be the perversion of the holy ones; this school of piety will become the model of every violence.

"Then, full of the disgust of things, man will no longer have for the world either admiration or love."

These studies, in which, as far as possible, we have allowed the Egyptians to speak for themselves, could not have a more fitting close than this pathetic and thrilling farewell addressed to the past by an Egyptian of the old school.

PRINCIPAL AUTHORITIES

Amélineau (E.), *Les nouvelles fouilles d'Abydos.* Paris.
Bouriant (U.), *Deux jours de fouilles à Tell el Amarna* (*Mémoires de la Mission archéologique français*), I. p. 1.
Brugsch (H.), *Reise nach der grossen Oase el-Khargeh.* Leipzig, 1878.
Capart (Jean), *Les débuts de l'art en Égypte.* Bruxelles, 1904.
Erman (A.), *Gespräch eines Lebensmüden mit seiner Seele.* Acad. des Sciences, Berlin, 1896.
Golénischeff (W.), *Die Metternichestele.* Leipzig, 1877.
Grebaut (E.), *Hymne à Ammon-Râ.* Bibliothèque de l'École des Hautes-Études, fasc. 21. Paris, 1875.
Jéquier (G.), *Le livre de ce qu'il y a dans l'Hades.* Paris, 1894.
Lefébure (E.), *Zeitsch. für aeg. Sprache.* 1883.
—— *Rites égyptiens.* Paris, 1890.
Mariette (A.), " Les tombes de l'Ancien Empire" (extrait de la *Revue archéologique*, 1868).
Maspero (G.), *The Life and Monuments of Thoutmôsis IV.*; in Th. Davis, *The Tomb of T. IV.* London, 1904.
—— *Études de mythologie et d'archéologie égyptiennes.* Vols. i. et ii. Paris.
—— *Les inscriptions des Pyramides de Saqqarah.* Paris, 1894.
—— *Le double et les statues prophétiques.* Études de mythologie. Vol. i.
—— *Les momies royales de Deir el Bahari* (*Mémoires de la Mission archéologique français*), I. p. 594.
Ménard (L.), *Hermès Trismégiste.* Paris, 1867.
Moret (A.), *Du caractère religieux de la royauté pharaonique.* Paris, 1902.
—— *Le rituel du culte divin journalier.* Paris, 1902.

PRINCIPAL AUTHORITIES 321

Morgan (J. de), *Recherches sur les origines de l'Égypte. L'âge de la pierre et les métaux.* Paris, 1896.
—— *Ethnographie préhistorique et tombeau royal de Negadah.* Paris, 1897.
Naville (E.), *The Temple of Deir el-Bahari.* Vols. ii. and iii.
—— *The Festival Hall of Osorkon II. in the Temple of Bubastis.* London, 1897.
—— *La destruction des hommes par les dieux (Trans. of S.B.A.,* 1875).
—— *A Mention of a Flood in the Book of the Dead (Trans. of S.B.A.,* 1904).
—— *Le chapitre 112 du Livre des Morts.* Études dediées à Leemans.
—— *Das aegyptische Todtenbuch der XVIII. bis XX. Dynastie,* Einleitung. Berlin, 1886.
—— *Inscription historique de Pinodjem III.* Paris, 1883.
—— *Les plus anciens monuments égyptiens (Recueil de travaux relatifs à la philologie et à l'archéologie égyptiennes et assyriennes,* vols. xxi., xxiv., and xxv.).
Petrie (Flinders), *Royal Tombs.* I., II. London, 1900.
—— *Abydos.* I., II., 1902-3.
Quibell (J. E.), *Hieraconpolis.* I., II. London, 1901-2.
Rougé (E. de), *Étude sur une stèle égyptienne, appartenant à la bibliothèque impériale.* Paris, 1858.
Le Page Renouf (P.), *The Egyptian Book of the Dead.* Translation and Commentary, continued by E. Naville.
Wiedemann (A.), *Religion of the Ancient Egyptians.* London, 1897.
—— *Menschenvergötterung im Alten Aegypten,* Urquell, Bd. VII. The same author in Morgan, *Recherches,* etc.

PRINTED BY NEILL AND CO., LTD., EDINBURGH.

www.ingramcontent.com/pod-product-compliance
Lightning Source LLC
Chambersburg PA
CBHW061247230426
43663CB00021B/2932